The Walled Gardens
of Herefordshire

The Walled Gardens of Herefordshire

edited by

Fiona Grant & Jane Patton

Hereford and Worcester Gardens Trust
in association with
Logaston Press

HEREFORD AND WORCESTER GARDENS TRUST

LOGASTON PRESS
Little Logaston Woonton Almeley
Herefordshire HR3 6QH
logastonpress.co.uk

First published 2009
Copyright © Hereford and Worcester Gardens Trust 2009

ISBN 978 1 906663 12 4

Typeset by Logaston Press
and printed and bound in Poland
www.polskabook.pl

Contents

Acknowledgements

The Hereford and Worcester Gardens Trust and the authors would like to thank the Ratcliffe Foundation for its generous grant towards this publication.

David Whitehead should like to acknowledge the generous help received for the chapter on George' Skippe's garden at Upper Hall from Mr. C.W. Johnson, the present owner of the garden, who guided him on the site and gave him access to his archive. His thanks go also to Mrs. Pat Strauss of Upper Hall, who made the introduction.

The relict walled gardens of both Old Sufton and Sufton Court were visited and Major and Mrs. James Hereford, the current owners were consulted, for which many thanks.

Fiona Grant should like to thank the late Mr. A.T. Foley for allowing access to the papers of the Foley Estate and permission to reproduce 'The Stag Hunt at Nieuport', and the present owners, Mr. and Mrs. Crichton-Watt, for their help and hospitality.

Editor's Preface

The Hereford and Worcester Gardens Trust has always encouraged research of the counties' historic gardens, as an essential part of the process of conservation: we must know what we have before we can conserve it.

In her foreword Susan Campbell has highlighted the current plight of walled gardens and the lack of data nationwide, with the exception of surveys carried out by one or two Garden Trusts. Such a survey can be a formidable task, but we are fortunate in Herefordshire to have the excellent *Survey of Historic Parks and Gardens of Herefordshire* by David Whitehead, edited by Jane Patton, which is a comprehensive survey of the county's historic gardens.

In Worcestershire Richard Lockett has laid the foundations of a similar survey, and it is proposed that he will resurvey his material for a subsequent publication based on the Herefordshire model. It was decided, therefore, to separate the publications on walled gardens. Since we had far more material for the Herefordshire survey, for reasons given above, it was decided that this should be published alone, with the intention of expanding the Worcestershire survey when Richard Lockett has completed his research, and bringing out a 'sister' publication at a later date.

Jane Patton had compiled a list of walled gardens, extrapolated from the Herefordshire Survey, and from this list we designed a further list with three columns for comments: condition; use, if any; any other comments. These were sent out to all the Trust's members, requesting their help in providing any information they could. We had a fantastic response, and I would like to take this opportunity to thank all those who took the time and trouble to respond, often providing copies of newspaper reports, photographs and maps. Without your help this survey could not have been achieved, and the result is a genuine group effort. However, the Trust cannot take responsibility for the accuracy of all the information. It has been checked as far as is reasonable, but there may well be inconsistencies due to subjective opinion or changes that have taken place since the survey. The Trust would, of course, welcome any corrections and additions, as we intend to keep the survey alive electronically and at some point a new edition may be deemed necessary. It should also be noted that the majority of these gardens are private and we request that the owners' rights to privacy be observed.

It was decided to include a number of studies on individual gardens of note, which would be representative of the present situation of walled gardens in a more national context. A range of different types of walled gardens in various stages of survival, from the historical investigation of some relict gardens to a flourishing example of a thriving community garden, makes up the main body of text.

The walled garden at Upper Hall, Ledbury is famous locally because of its appearance in the diary of its late 17th-century owner, George Skippe. The diary reveals something of the pristine glory of the garden and subsequent documents bring the story up to date. Remarkably, notwithstanding local rumours to the contrary, it survives today virtually intact beneath a spreading canopy of woodland.

Sufton Court, near Hereford, has the vestiges of two walled gardens. Both belong to the Hereford family who came to Sufton in the 13th century and thrive there today. The walled garden at Old Sufton with its summerhouse/dovecote, perched on a rock, may have been known in the late 17th century by John Evelyn via his local correspondent John Beale. It survived because in 1788 a new house was built elsewhere on the estate, which was provided with a Repton landscape and a new walled garden.

Downton Castle has one of those rare walled gardens which are linked with famous names in garden history, and in this case with two. Laid out by Richard Payne Knight when he built the castle in the late 18th century, it was later used as a site for horticultural experiments when his brother Thomas Andrew Knight, by then an established horticultural scientist, inherited the estate.

The walled garden at Nieuport House is an encouraging success story of a garden rescued from dereliction. After nearly ninety years of council ownership, it is now being meticulously restored and brought back to life by the new owner, who intends to grow fruit and vegetables organically, using the traditional layout.

The garden at Haffield is a privately owned garden with Loudon associations that has been in continuous production since its inception in the early 19th century. It is a double-walled garden, which is comparatively rare, but even more unusual is the mysterious tunnel that connects it to the pleasure gardens adjoining the house, which was designed in 1818 by Sir Robert Smirke.

Lugwardine Court is a shining example of how a walled garden can be found an appropriate new role for the 21st century. The charity Workmatch has taken on a long term lease and has restored the walls and structures with HLF funding. The garden now provides education and training for the disadvantaged and the long term unemployed. Walled gardens are of course ideal for this purpose as they provide a private and secure environment.

This book is very much a collaborative effort, and I would like to thank all the authors for their excellent contributions. I would also like to thank the Hereford and Worcester Gardens Trust for their generous support and constant faith in the project, and in particular Jane Patton for her meticulous editing of the survey. We are most grateful to the owners of these gardens for their cooperation in allowing access and for their help towards the research.

Fiona Grant, October 2007

Foreword

For those who love walled gardens — and walled kitchen gardens in particular — their past neglect by garden historians can only be explained by a value system that places the productive garden far lower down the scale than the designed landscape. They are, moreover, rarely associated with famous names in garden history. In this way, walled gardens might be seen as the Cinderellas of that subject. But they still have a fascinating story to tell: of skilled gardeners providing the family with the finest fruit and vegetables throughout the year, of ingenious glasshouses, pits and frames where fruit and vegetables could be induced to ripen out of season, and of back-sheds, storage rooms and bothies in which past generations of gardener's boys, apprentices and journeymen worked and lived.

One consequence of historians' assessment of their value and interest has been that these walled gardens are often neglected, even as a category on their own, in surveys of gardens of historic interest. They can all too easily fall through the net, and consequently they do not always receive the attention that they deserve. As they have never been the subject of a national survey in this country, the number of surviving walled gardens is mainly guesswork, but there must be thousands. Many are derelict with crumbling walls, the glasshouses collapsed and overgrown, and the once neat rows of vegetables and espaliered fruit trees overrun with brambles and weeds. In this state they are vulnerable to development, and while some development can ensure their survival, there are far too many examples of unsuitable and unsympathetic schemes, often in the form of high-density housing.

However, there are signs that this imbalance is to be addressed. English Heritage is in the process of producing a HELM (Historic Environment Local Management) publication on walled kitchen gardens, and some Garden Trusts, such as Hampshire, have already produced surveys of those in their county.

I am delighted that the Hereford and Worcester Gardens Trust is following suit, and I take great satisfaction in writing the foreword to this book, which is the fruit of some of the Trust's painstaking research.

Susan Campbell, August 2007

Notes on Contributors

Francesca Bingham studied at the University of Bristol and took an MA in Landscape and Garden History in 2005. Since then, she has worked for the National Trust and freelanced as a lecturer and archivist. Her particular interest is in the 20th century and especially the inter-war and post-war periods, which for walled garden history has been a period of intense alteration and also restoration. Francesca is always interested in researching gardens and enjoys giving talks and garden tours.

Magda Boucher trained and worked as an archaeologist for a number of years before moving to Herefordshire and retraining in Horticulture. She has worked as a gardener and horticultural therapist (having completed the Diploma in Therapeutic Horticulture with Coventry University). Magda also has an interest in garden history, and in growing old varieties of plants and vegetables.

Jane Bradney is a garden historian with a special interest in the 19th century. She has lectured for the National Trust, County Gardens Trusts and a range of specialist interest groups. Her article, 'The Carriage Drives of Sir Humphry Repton', was published in *Garden History* in 2005. She was awarded an MA in Garden History at the University of Bristol in 2004 where she is currently researching the Italian Garden in England from 1784 to 1863 for a doctoral thesis. She lives in south Herefordshire.

Susan Campbell has been researching the history of the walled kitchen garden for nearly 20 years. She has personally visited and photographed nearly 500 walled kitchen gardens in the UK and abroad, and is a foremost authority on the subject. She has published several books on the subject and lectures and advises professionally. She is chairman for the Walled Kitchen Gardens Network.

Fiona Grant has a background in the history of art and design and is now a garden historian with a particular interest in walled kitchen gardens. She was instrumental in founding the Walled Kitchen Gardens Network, a voluntary association that offers support and advice to those who wish to conserve these gardens. Fiona also lectures on garden history and regularly organises and leads garden tours for the public. She now acts as secretary for the Network.

Dr. Murray Mylechreest is an Honorary Research Fellow of the University of Worcester who has researched the life and contributions to science and horticulture of Thomas Andrew Knight for several years, with publication of papers and presentations for national and international conferences. His interest in horticultural science was the basis of a career in education, having established a degree in horticulture at the University of Worcester in conjunction with Pershore College.

Jane Patton is a landscape architect who worked for the Conservation and Environmental Planning Department of Herefordshire Council for a number of years. She is a long standing committee member of the Hereford and Worcester Gardens Trust and editor of their newsletter. Historic parks and gardens, and especially walled gardens, have always held a special interest for her and while working in Herefordshire she became familiar with most of the historic gardens in the county. She recognised that Herefordshire has a particularly rich heritage of surviving historic parks and gardens and has always dreamt that one day they would become as celebrated as those of Cornwall.

David Whitehead has lived and taught in Hereford for most of his working life, lecturing and writing extensively on many aspects of the man-made landscape. Recently, he has found that garden history, in the evenings, perfectly complements the sunny days he spends working in his own semi-walled suburban garden. He is a member of many national and local societies devoted to history and the environment, and is also a fellow of the Society of Antiquaries.

Introduction

My memories of the long hot summer of 1977 are grounded in the delightful but dishevelled garden of a great friend. Heavily pregnant, I spent my waiting hours encircled by the old brick walls, hidden behind the gothic wooden doors in a languid world of fragrant colour and teeming life. The mental filmstrip of that summer comes back to me whenever I visit or think of a walled garden — and who amongst us could say that they were any more impervious to their allure? Who can resist the frisson of excitement when faced with the closed inwardly-opening door, or the clutter of gardening debris amongst the tumbledown sheds on the wrong side of the wall? The seduction of the walled garden conquers us all, young and old, readers of Frances Hodgson Burnett's *Secret Garden* or not. They are hidden private places where anything might be found and where we can retreat from the real world, indulging our need for solitude, fantasy and, sometimes, hard work.

So it is that over many years of working as a landscape architect my love of walled gardens has been nourished by a stream of visits, both for work and play. When the Hereford and Worcester Gardens Trust decided to sponsor this book about the walled gardens of Herefordshire, I was delighted to be asked to write an introduction.

There were never any truly palatial houses in Herefordshire, but the county was very well served with comfortable gentry estates. Every estate had its large mansion, and every village had at least one imposing house, and these were all set within the gardens and parkland that have made Herefordshire famously so attractive. In fact, the estates were so numerous that one ran into another throughout most of the county, with the commons and occasional small farms between. Throughout the last few centuries, wealthy landowners have put their money into their rural property to create the fashionable gardens that would reflect their status and wealth. Walled gardens were part of this enthusiasm for creating the perfect country idyll and in a county that hosted the two protagonists of the picturesque movement, Uvedale Price at Foxley and Richard Payne Knight at Downton, the interest in all things gardenesque was intense. The development of orcharding, encouraged by Herefordshire's fertile soils and generous climate, and aided by the likes of Thomas Andrew Knight, the second president of the Royal Horticultural Society, also encouraged the creation of walled gardens. Indeed, one of the finest walled gardens, with the original range of glasshouses in which Knight carried out his celebrated orchard breeding, is still in good condition at Downton Castle.

A few years ago, while carrying out some preliminary research for David Whitehead's *Historic Parks and Gardens in Herefordshire* (2001), I visited almost all the historic gardens in Herefordshire and made a note of which ones included a walled garden. Then some time later an exciting new grant came into being, funded by European Union money and administered by the usual environmental quangos. It looked ideal for the basis of a project to help the restoration and secure the future use of at least some of the walled gardens and so I embarked on a fascinating journey of discovery as I revisited numerous gardens to eventually come up with my list of the ten most deserving cases. Herefordshire Council, my employer at the time, were very supportive of the whole idea and the future looked very promising for the chosen few. Sadly, the grant never materialised and no explanation was ever given. No doubt it fell back into the black hole of EU finance. Luckily the owners had not made any financial commitment by the time that the plug was pulled but they all had a very disappointing Christmas and I felt so sorry to have to break the bad news to them at such a festive season. The experience has, however, left me feeling that I probably know more about the walled gardens of Herefordshire than almost anyone else. The range of design is extraordinary: from the vast to the tiny; from the geometric to the free-form; from gardens of a commercial scale to the little flower garden; with stone or brick walls; with fascinating garden features and ancillary buildings; and spanning several centuries.

The popular concept of a walled garden is probably a high brick wall enclosing a square area that is divided by two crossing paths into quadrants of equal size. A circular pool will be situated in the centre, where the paths cross, and a peripheral path will run round the encircling wall that has espaliered fruit trees trained against it. One wall will be covered in lean-to glasshouses and there will be a range of small buildings such as a potting shed, mushroom house and wood store along the outside of another wall. There will be at least two doors into the garden, usually painted an attractive mossy green. The gardeners will grow serried ranks of vegetables and one quadrant may house orchard trees with perhaps an apple arch along the central paths. Certainly this idealised concept has its basis in fact and there were many walled gardens in Herefordshire

Plate I. The bothy in the wall of the garden at Clater Park

that would have conformed to this description. The walled garden at Moccas, for example, would have been such a garden. When I visited it a few years ago the wall was intact and the mossy green doors were firmly shut against all-comers, for the interior was so closely packed with overgrown Christmas trees, planted for a long-ago market and somehow overlooked, that one could barely squeeze through them to discover that everything else in the garden had been removed. The trees are now being cleared and there are plans to restore the garden to productivity, although the paths and the central dipping pool may have to wait a little longer.

As fascinating as gardens like Moccas are, the unusual, idiosyncratic gardens are of even more interest. The smallest walled garden in the county must be the little walled enclosure at Clater Park, where the brick wall is a sinuous curve on one side and has been taken down on another to open up the view. The resulting lopsided ovoid shape is relieved by a tiny bothy set into one of the only straight sections of wall. It has a tiny doorway and two little gothic windows that open into a space so small that it can barely accommodate two seated persons at a time. There is a little open grate set into the wall and a ladder leading to an upstairs room, equally small with even less headroom under a pitched roof (Plate I).

At the opposite extreme is the vast walled garden at Goodrich, with its complete range of potting sheds along the outside of the northern wall. The walled gardens at Berrington Hall and Croft Castle are also extensive, with one of the foremost collections of old apple varieties being housed at Berrington and spectacular displays of perennial planting delighting visitors at Croft.

Generally, the walls around the gardens are constructed of brick, with a brick or tile coping, but this is not always so. The walled garden at Birchyfield, on the outskirts of Bromyard, is in a sadly dilapidated state and from the outside it is apparent that the walls are mainly made of stone, with vast buttresses several metres high (Plate II). To stand in the field with the walls soaring above one's head is an awesome experience. Within the walled garden there are also a number of garden structures that, sadly, are deteriorating fast. The summerhouse is particularly appealing, with its original Georgian panelling, staircase and window seats. In some gardens the walls are just part of a more complex built system. Haffield, which is described in this book, has a unique approach through a tunnel built into the wall, and Kinnersley Castle has a partially hedged ante-chamber so that the visitor enters a separate walled enclosure before gaining entry to the walled garden proper.

Typically, other walled garden structures would include a range of glasshouses built to house citrus fruits and extend the growing season. These have always been costly to maintain and were often the first to go when a garden was deteriorating. Nevertheless there are gardens where the glasshouses have been well maintained or restored. Hampton Court garden, where so much exemplary restoration work has been carried out, has a range of greenhouses that have been completely restored. Great care has been taken to ensure that the restoration is in keeping. All the brass fixtures and fittings have been replaced with similar ones, hardwood timber has been used from the estate and even the glass has been repaired correctly, using hand-made glass from Poland that gives the same quality of light as the original. In other gardens pineapple pits and the original watering and heating systems are still in use. At The Weir, the National Trust are in the process of restoring their walled garden and have started by fully restoring the greenhouses.

Plate II. The outside of the walled garden at Birchyfield, near Bromyard

Many of the walled gardens are derelict but many are well used and still fulfilling their original role of producing fruit, vegetables and cut flowers. Some, like the garden at Whitfield with its original camellia house complete with ancient camellias, still supply the big house. Some, like the small garden at Titley Court, supply the local pubs and restaurants. Many, however, like the garden at Lawton, near Leominster, have all but disappeared. The large house that it once must have served is long gone and all that remains is a lofty stone wall, supported incongruously by timber props in a grassy meadow. The farmhouse nearby, where the owners run a thriving herb business, is called Lawton Hall, possibly a reference to the long-lost original house. The walled garden is a walk away through the meadows towards its lonely companion wall. Its own walls have tumbled down or disappeared but the idea is to rebuild them or at least to plant their outline with windbreak hedges, as the garden's situation is ideal for plant growth and an extension of the business.

Most of the gardens date from the late 18th century. They were genrally used to grow fruit, vegetables and cut flowers and were sited at a distance from the main house as they were perceived as the working part of the estate. Some, however, were designed as a garden enclosure for the house. The Georgian walled garden at Wormsley Grange was built as a flower garden and laid out in a formal style. The Grange and its delightful garden are now being restored by new owners. The concept of a walled garden could also be extended to include other domestic gardens such as the 20th century Italianate garden at How Caple Court or the very early flower garden at Hall Court, Kynaston, which probably dates from the early 17th century. Another very ancient site, which can easily be seen from the road to Mordiford, is the irregular enclosure at Old Sufton which is located on a south facing hillside to maximise the warmth of the sunshine. The site was first mentioned as a garden by John Evelyn in the mid 17th century. The walls and the summerhouse and dovecote are Georgian, dating from the early 18th century.

The future of Herefordshire's walled gardens has looked bleak for a number of years as walls have collapsed, gardens have run wild and their large houses have struggled to keep out the rain. Many gardens have been irrevocably lost, like those on the edge of Ross-on-Wye where developers have built high density housing with little regard to any alternative potential for the walled gardens. The last few years, however, have seen a resurgence of interest in all gardens and the romance of walled gardens has stood them in good stead with potential restorers. Many of the gardens that I originally viewed without much hope for their future are now thriving, or at least their future is secured. Perhaps the most successful story is the garden at Lugwardine, which has been restored by volunteers from a not-for-profit organisation and now offers work opportunities for people with learning difficulties. At Harewood End the walled garden that was infamously used to breed beagles for scientific research will now be restored by the Duchy of Cornwall, who intend to use it for soft fruit production, contributing to their Duchy Originals range of jams and preserves. At Homme House the Watch Tower, an eccentric two storey stone gazebo built into the corner of the wall (Plate III), has been rescued from collapse and plans are in hand to bring the

Plate III. The Watch Tower in the garden at Homme House

garden back to productivity. Other gardens have, ironically, been saved by development. Several, like Hope End and Brockhampton, are now the private garden of a single house built inside the wall, or converted from the original garden buildings. Although sometimes a controversial solution, it does guarantee the garden's survival and for many gardens may be the optimal answer to the intractable problem of maintaining a walled garden that no longer has an obvious function.

The walled gardens described in this book are but the tip of an iceberg, and I do not claim that even the list of walled gardens at the end of this book is exhaustive. In fact, I would be most surprised if no others were to come to light. I hope that all the prominent gardens are covered but no doubt the discerning reader will know of other deserving gardens that have been overlooked. The Hereford and Worcester Gardens Trust would be delighted to hear from anyone who could contribute additional entries.

George Skippe and his Walled Garden at Upper Hall, Ledbury

One of the minor inconveniences of garden history is to find a splendid relict landscape which on further enquiries lacks documentary sources. Perhaps even more disappointing is the reverse situation: to come across a manuscript describing a much-loved garden which no longer exists. The diary of George Skippe, to be found in the library of the Woolhope Naturalists Field Club, locked away in a strongbox in the vaults of the Hereford City Library, seemed just such a source.[1] The diary, or more accurately the commonplace book, records the financial dealings of a member of a minor gentry family who lived at Upper Hall, Ledbury in the late 17th century (Fig. 1). Deeply embedded in the manuscript are occasional references to national and local events and, more specifically, an account of the building, stocking and management of a walled garden.

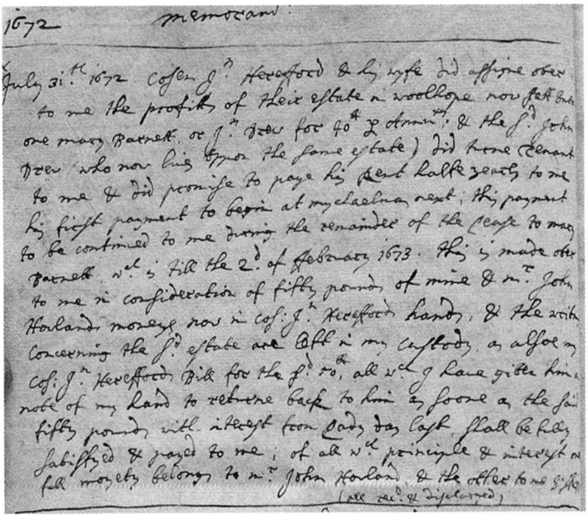

Fig. 1. A typical page in the diary

Preliminary enquiries suggested that the garden had disappeared when the Skippe mansion became a state school in the 1920s. A sale catalogue of 1919 shows a modest enclosure with greenhouses behind the stable block, which is described as 'a high walled-in kitchen garden'. It was subsequently used for classrooms and is now occupied by a large single-storey dwelling built in the 1990s. The garden described in the diary had, it seems, disappeared.

The Skippes acquired Upper Hall in the late 16th century. It was originally a 'portionist' estate supporting the churchmen who served in the ancient minster church at Ledbury — hence its proximity, immediately to the north.[2] George Skippe (1623-90) recorded in his diary that his father John assigned Upper Hall to him in 1662, but he did not move into the house until 1670 when his father took up residence at Wall Hills, a satellite estate held by the family to the west of Ledbury, where he died in 1684. George inherited a substantial timber-framed house to which his father had added a new brick wing, on the south-western side of the central hall, some time around 1660 (Plate I).[3] Apart from Wall Hills, the family owned many small parcels of land around Ledbury and a town house in London. A substantial part of George's income came from industrial and commercial ventures in Bristol, Kidderminster, Gloucestershire and elsewhere, as well as his informal role as a banker, lending money far and wide, in Herefordshire and beyond. The purpose of his diary, which was kept from 1668 until his death in 1690, was to record these transactions, but like all regular diary keepers he frequently ventured into other aspects of his daily life.

Plate I. The c.1660 wing of Upper Hall to the left of the later Georgian/Victorian mansion

He comes across as a methodical and shrewd businessman. He was always fair but rarely generous and even his financial dealings with his immediate family were recorded with the same discipline he employed with strangers. He was constantly serving the debts of his younger brother 'Dick' and equally fastidious in his financial relations with his father. Sadly, although he was clearly fascinated by the world around him, this kind of remark only forms a minor part of his diary and is often rather cursory. He notices, for instance, the floods and storms of December 1672, when the 'Severn and other Rivers in these parts were extremely out, further than they were ever known before in the memory of man'. On 29 August 1683 he experienced a 'great earthquake' sitting in his summerhouse 'betwixt 9 and 10 of the clocke … the room moved violently, there being no wind then'. There were further weaker shocks later in the same autumn. All, it seems, was not well with the world, and nearby in the diary, Skippe records that the Turkish army was camped before Vienna, posing a great threat, it seemed, to European civilisation. Skippe recorded that the 'great frost' — also noticed by John Evelyn in 1683 — began on 15 December and continued until 5 February, when it was followed by 'great snow'.[4]

Skippe was a countryman at heart, owning several horses and a succession of hawks. In July 1682 he made a new fishpond on Stony Hill, fenced it around and stocked it with 62 carp, tench and perch from Eastnor. He was very conscious of the changing seasons and records random incidents such as on 18 January 1675: 'I heard a chaffinch singing at Over (Upper) hall' and three years earlier, on February 13 1672: 'I heard a wild blackbird sing on Robberts Hill'. Again, on 25 March 1683, 'about this time I sate several dayes in the arbour in the vinyard & a robin redbreast did there eat out of my hand & sate on my foote'. A particularly reflective entry occurs on 11 May 1675: 'Being Tuesday my wife walked up to the top of Bradley Hill at sunset and was afterwards delivered of a daughter'. She was baptised Elizabeth in Ledbury church the following Sunday when, rather symbolically, Skippe noted 'I did gather 7 ripe cherries in my new garden'. He now had four living children.[5]

The 'new garden' figured regularly in Skippe's diary from September 1671 when he 'agreed with William Higgins of Worcester for the making of 40,000 bricks in Holborn Croft at 4s 6d per 1000'. The Croft was above the house on the open pasture beneath Dog Hill Wood. At the same time Skippe employed two craftsmen, Mr. Colcott and Mr. Fisher, 'for finishing the garden wall' in return for £40. Built close to the wall was a new stable block, erected by William Morse and his men, assisted by Colcott and John Richards, a carpenter. As Colcott and Fisher were 'finishing the garden wall' it seems likely that the wall had been commenced sometime before, perhaps by Skippe's father. The brick kiln in Holborn Croft was working for eight months and Higgins was paid off in May 1672. However, in the summer of 1674 his son Jack appears in the diary and contracts to make 30,000 bricks to enclose a bowling green. This was a joint endeavour undertaken by Skippe and his neighbour at Little Marcle, Sir Thomas Hanbury. The site of the bowling green is not known but it seems unlikely that it was at Upper Hall.[6]

That Higgins came from Worcester is no surprise for although brick was a relatively new material in the West Midlands in the late 17th century, Worcester had a brick and tile industry that stretched back into the Middle Ages.[7] Probably the principal use of brick in Ledbury in this period was to top-off chimneys. In 1587 Edward Cooper, the Master of St Katherine's Hospital in Ledbury, obtained brick for this purpose from Hanley Castle, where it had probably been brought down the river from Worcester.[8] Mr. Colcott was a carpenter from London. (This is mentioned in connection with the record of his being paid-off in August 1672.) He worked on the stable block, the 'bottle house' — mentioned in April 1672 — and probably the summerhouse built in the north-east corner of the walled garden. Fisher was presumably a mason/bricklayer and seems to have come from Hereford, where his family worked in and around the cathedral during this period. For similar reasons it can be assumed that Richards, the other carpenter, came from Worcester.[9] Some of these craftsmen may have worked on the south range of the house, which, it has been assumed, was built a little earlier and contains a fine staircase, worthy of Colcott's metropolitan connections. There is no indication in the diary, however, that the mansion was undergoing extensive work at this time.

Notwithstanding the widely held view that Skippe's walled garden had disappeared in the early 20th century, a major part of it still survives, terraced into the south-western slopes of Dog Hill. Although the longest walls were on the north and west, it was conveniently tipped-up to provide good drainage and absorb the maximum amount of sunlight. The slope at the top of the garden, below the summerhouse in its north-east corner,

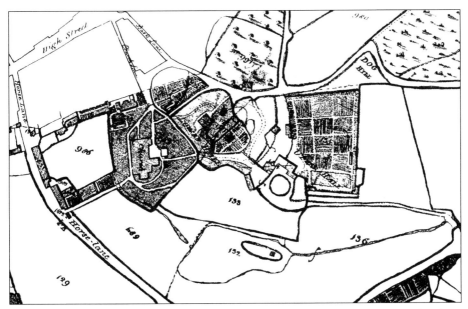

*Fig. 2. A section of the Ledbury Tithe Map (1841) showing the grounds of
Upper Hall with the walled garden indicated with plots and rows*

is decidedly precipitous. The garden is depicted at its full extent on the
Ledbury Enclosure Map (1816) and on the Tithe Map (1841) (Fig. 2).[10]
Measurements taken from these plans suggest that it was 110 yards by
60, making it 6,600 square yards, well over an acre in extent. Today
there are walls on the north and west but an estate plan by Robert Jones
of 1843, perhaps based upon the Tithe Map, shows buildings against a
wall on the east, perhaps the bothies, forcing houses etc.[11] used by the
gardeners. On the south the garden was open and was overlooked by the
north and west frontage of the mansion. The ground was scarped and
held in place by a stone wall. The odd relationship between the Hall and
its garden emphasises the late arrival of the latter but Skippe was probably aware that the full glory of the garden would be revealed from the
first-floor rooms — the *piano nobile* in current Italianate perceptions. Jean
de La Quintinye (or perhaps his translator, John Evelyn) recommended
the 'perpetual Action of the Gard'ners' as an entertaining diversion, if
the garden was visible from the house.[12] No doubt Skippe's five daugh-
ters were enthralled! A similar relationship between house and garden
existed a few miles away at Old Colwall where brick walls and enclo-
sures are at first-floor level, but unlike Skippe's garden, on a horizontal
plane.[13] Another feature Upper Hall shared with Old Colwall was a

'great gate' flanked by two piers, erected by Fisher and his men for £3 10s. in December 1671. It is difficult to imagine where this feature stood, but given the later east-west axis of the garden, a position in the middle of the east wall would have been most convenient and grand.

Although by the late 17th century the separation of the kitchen garden from the pleasure garden was well advanced for great houses, for the lesser gentry the walled enclosure still served a dual purpose.[14] Soon after Skippe completed his garden he added Leonard Meager's *The English Gardner* (1676), to his library (Fig. 3). This was a popular book, reaching twelve editions by 1721, but also old-fashioned, suggesting a homely mixture of fruit and flowers within the same enclosure. One of Meager's primary recommendations was certainly taken by Skippe, namely, 'In the first place, you are if you may conveniently, to erect (the Garden of Pleasure) in such a place where it may yield most delight, in regard of its prospect from your House, or some chief Rooms thereof'. Having suggested 'diverse sorts' of roots, herbs and flowers, enclosed by box, he has little to say about the planning of the garden 'but only that you would be careful so to fit your work to your ground, that it may lie pleasant and suitable, not too thick, but so as there may be convenient to pass to every part of your work'. He provides 24 plans which, apart from one with a complex design for 'Wilderness Worke', are based upon the square or rectangle and thus, could easily be 'fitted for the use of all such as delight in Gardening'. At least two of these are based upon a central oval and bear some resemblance to the garden that was mapped in 1843 (Fig. 4). Much of the advice about propagation and cultivation would, no doubt, have appealed to Skippe. For example, it was best to water in the evening with pond or ditch water; to have 'some great Tubs fill'd, wherein they put Sheeps dung or other dung, letting it stand in the Sun until it is in a

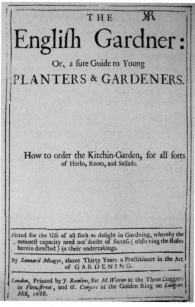

Fig. 3. The title page of The English Gardener *(1688). Skippe probably had an earlier edition in his library*

14

better case to use' and to have ample sage and rosemary beds 'to be cut smooth and handsome ... They will be useful as an Hedge to lay small Cloaths upon to white or dry, besides a handsome Ornament in a Garden'. There is much more besides.[15] Watering a steeply sloping garden was clearly a problem and it was not until 1690 that Peter Bullock 'finished his work in drawing the water to the Cistern in the garden at the Hall'. Oak, elm and cherry wood were used in the various parts of the work.

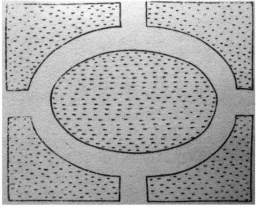

Fig. 4. One of Meager's simple plans for a garden. The oval design appears at the top of Skippe's garden enclosure in the early 19th century

How did Skippe plant and develop his new garden? In November 1672 he hired Symon Bayly as 'my Gardener', offering to pay him £10 per annum with an additional five shillings paid 'towards his charges from London'. Skippe maintained strong business connections with the metropolis, having lived in Chelsea before moving to Ledbury in 1670. Thus, he may have recruited Bayly, as an experienced gardener, specifically to lay out and plant his new brick enclosure. We learn little about his activities but Skippe notices in passing in 1683 that Bayly raised two walnuts, which were then flourishing 'in the brick garden'. He may not have stayed very long for in March 1674, Skippe drew up new articles with Mr. Wilton 'the Gardener for his servant Roger Cheeseman to come an live with me on 25th May'. He was to pay him £11 for a year and a half, which suggests he was to be an under-gardener. A year later he was hired as a full-time gardener at £6 per annum. This was considerably less than Bayly's annual wage and perhaps emphasises the latter's pre-eminence as a professional. Additionally, Cheeseman occasionally fired-up Skippe's brick kiln and was given an extra 6d. for every pound's worth of 'brick, tyles and other wares he sells for me'. In November 1682 Skippe hired Thomas Yeoman as his gardener at 3s. per week, which seems a good wage. However, in order to defray this regular payment Skippe encouraged Yeoman to set up beehives in the garden. When he had established 50 'flocks' (swarms?) his wages would stop, presumably because he could make a good income from selling honey. Nevertheless, the hardworking beekeeper was 'to look after the whole work of the brick garden and what he can more of the other gardens, and to teach Moses Greenway the whole art of gardening'. The latter remained with Skippe until the late 1680s and Thomas Greenway, perhaps his son, was still employed by Skippe's widow in 1697.[16] Other labourers were sometimes employed on an irregular basis, for instance, in August 1673 'John Jones was working in my new Garden at the Hall and recd. a hurt in his belly against the hinder part of the Hand barrow, of wch. he dyed the next daye'.

Since Skippe's diary is principally concerned with financial matters, it is not surprising that the coming and going of his gardeners is well recorded. We might expect details of his purchases — seeds, plants, equipment etc. — but of this, there is no trace. If Skippe followed Leonard Meager's old-fashioned ideas, he probably developed a mixed garden — productive as well as beautiful — with the most pleasing part of the garden close to the house and 'such as might offend the sight or smell, most at a distance'. John Rea, who lived a few miles away in south Shropshire, recommended a discreet painted wooden pale to separate the two parts of the garden.[17] But this is conjecture. To return to the diary, we learn that in March 1672 Skippe's wife planted two pots of 'Lucibells viz Balsome' in the garden beneath their chamber window. 'Lucibells' could be the local name for Lily of the Valley (*Convallaria majalis*), and with its strong perfume this would be well placed beneath a bedroom window and, according to Gerard and Parkinson, had many other 'virtues'. But it is by no means a balsam, which most obviously would seem to be Bee Balm (*Melissa officinalis*). Again this came highly recommended by the 17th-century herbalists. Just as Skippe noticed the seasonal changes in the weather and the unusual behaviour of birds, so on 19 February 1673 he recorded that he had gathered 'a full blown Red Rose' from his garden in Ledbury.

Such is the sparse information on the floristry at Upper Hall contained in George Skippe's diary. Fortunately, the diary is much more forthcoming on the productive aspects of the garden. In February 1687 Skippe decided to make a note on the progress of his asparagus, a popular and varied vegetable by the late 17th century. Like many of his contemporaries (and, indeed, gardeners today), he was trying to

16

extend the period of cropping.[18] He had planted his first asparagus at the Vineyard at Wall Hills in the spring of 1684. In August 1686 more plants were set out below the Steward's House, perhaps at Upper Hall, where the final planting also took place in February 1687. Clearly Skippe had a well-developed appetite for asparagus, although some of it may have been destined for the market place.

His most revealing enthusiasm was for his fruit trees. When Symon Bayly arrived from London in 1672 he was 'sent down with fruit trees to plant in my new garden'. These were clearly flourishing in September 1679 when Sam Mosse was paid 3s 6d. for leather 'for nailing up my garden trees for the year now ending'. Later, in November 1681, Skippe 'sett 35 pear trees at the new daye house', which may have been among the outhouses clustered at the bottom of the walled garden. Significantly, perhaps, this was the year T. Langford published the *Plain and full instructions to raise all sorts of fruit trees* (1681) which, according to the catalogue of books attached to the diary, was to be found in Skippe's library. The position of the new orchard is perhaps clarified in 1683 when Skippe stated 'I planted the new orchard by the brick garden partly in the winter of 1681 and the rest in 1682'. This suggests that the site was outside the walled garden, perhaps adjoining the north wall, where an orchard existed in the 19th century.

In a separate appendix to the diary Skippe lists 'The names of the wall Fruit in my new garden at Ledbury to begin from the great double doors & soe by the paving steps. viz. (by what names I bought them) (Fig. 5)':

From the doors downwards viz.

1. The Golden Peach
2. The Argier Apricock
3. The Lukeward Cherry
4. The Newington nectorine
5. The superintendant peach
6. The early Apricocke
7. The Duke cherry
8. The Roman red nectorine
9. The Magration plum
10. The Virgillo pear
11. The Newington peach
12. The Carnation cherry
13. The Roman Apricocke

1. The Black Hart cherry
2. The White Hart cherry
3. The may cherry
4. The persian nectorine
5. The early (double) apricocke
6. The orleance peach
7. The Admirable peach
8. The Brown nutmeg peach
9. The Holland plum
10. The jarsey peach
11. The Duke cherry
12. The murry nectorine
13. The Argier apricock

14. The Scarlet peach
15. The morello cherry
16. The murry nectorine
17. The Morocco (suske) plum
18. The Savoye peach
19. The Martin sack pear
20. The Bellose peach
21. The Russett petty black pear
22. The French morel plum

14. The Duke cherry
15. The Alburye peach
16. The navar peach
17. The Monsieur Johnpear
18. The ring pear
19. The rombullion peach
20. The Newington peach
21. White nutmeg peach
22. The Colux peach

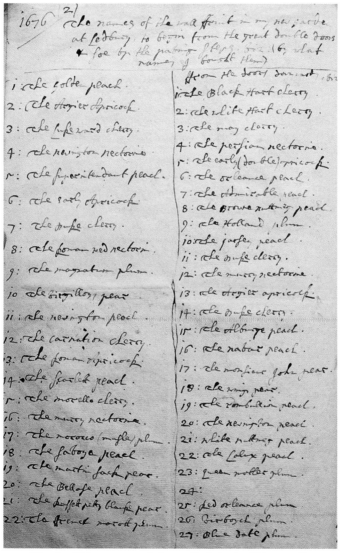

Fig. 5. 'The names of the wall fruit' in Skippe's diary

23. Queen noller plum
24. (Blank)
25. Red orleance plum
26. Virboych plum
27. Blue date plum

The names of the wall fruit trees in the inward new garden viz:

Next the doore entering into the garden are:

1. Bleeding Hart cherry
2. Morocco plum
3. Persian peach
4. Fower may cherryes

on the wall in the melon ground

1. Savoye (or yellow) peach
2. Burederoye peach
3. Winter buncrittion pear
4. Syon peach
5. Elruge nectorine
6. Violett muske peach
7. Roman red nectorine
8. Roman red nectorine
9. Mussle plum

There is an additional list in different handwriting, presumably that of George Skippe's son, John:

The names of my Wall fruit bought in the year 1705 part of which is set nye green walk to begin from ye top so towards ye house.

1. Muscatt pear
2. White Figg
3. Chesin plum
4. Brussells apricock
5. Admirable peach
6. Bellsheverus peach
7. Admirable peach
8. Bellsheverus peach
9. White Magdelin peach
10. Blew Pergrigon plum
11. White Pergrigon plum
12. Bury pear
13. Blanquet pear
14, 15, & 16. Three old plum trees
17. White Magdalin peach
18. Burgundi grape

Two violet Brugnon peach
Murry nectorin
Pearll grape

These last mentioned are taken into ye wall garden

In total the number of different kind of fruit mentioned were: peaches 22, plums 12, pears 9, cherries 8, nectarines 5, apricots 5, grapes 2 and figs 1.

The unregulated proliferation of named fruit trees in the late 17th century is a well-recorded phenomenon and Skippe's parenthesis '(by what names I bought them)' suggests that he was aware that new names did not necessarily mean new varieties. Stephen Switzer commented on the multiplication of varieties and noticed that half of La Quintine's book was taken up with a catalogue of fruit. Skippe's list was studied by Edward Ball in 1954.[19] Using two or three near-contemporary books he was only able to locate eleven peaches, six plums, seven pears, three nectarines, one apricot, the fig and all eight of the cherries. Only a small minority of these survived until the mid 20th century. Among these were the peach Admirable, two apricots — the Brussels and White, three plums — the Morocco, Mussle and White Pergrigon, the Bury pear, possibly six cherries and two of the nectarines, one of which had been recommended by Leonard Meager and, perhaps, caught Skippe's attention. In a postscript to Ball's article a Mr. A. Simmons of the RHS comments on the large number of peaches — two more than the 21 listed by Parkinson in *Paradisi in Sole* (1629). He concludes: 'I doubt whether many gardens of the period could have had so many plums or cherries. (As for) the pears he does not seem to have been very strong for Parkinson listed 63'.

In the midst of his orchard adjoining the 'brick garden' Skippe placed four walnut trees. Two of these had been raised by Bayly, whilst the other two were set in 1682. One came from William Baldwin, the other had been raised by Skippe himself from a 'double walnut I had from the Beck meadow'. The 'double walnut' was probably *Juglans nigra* from Virginia, which had been introduced in 1629. The fruits of this variety are carried in pairs. Incidentally, he reflects that two further walnuts had been set by himself in 1654 at the Vineyard and the Washing Pool at Wall Hills, which he subsequently transplanted to Upper Hall. Skippe's enthusiasm for the walnut probably derived from John Evelyn's *Sylva*, which was also in his well-stocked library.[20]

From July 1680 Skippe regularly recorded his winemaking activities, using currants, gooseberries and red and white grapes. On 9 July 1686, for example, the pressed currants made 104 gallons of must. This was fermented with Lisbon sugar — purchased from Gloucester — and put through a sieve to remove the remaining impurities. To enrich the vintage a gallon of 'raspberry ground' was added to the mix. Two days later 64 pounds of gooseberries were pressed and sugar added. Both wines were racked into new barrels in September. Some of the containers were homemade while others were bought from John Cox in Gloucester and since Skippe gave some of the barrels to his brother Dick, who was presumably also a domestic wine-maker. White grapes were also pressed and produced four dozen bottles of wine, which, in the following March were given more body by the addition of 'Raisins of the Sun'. The red grapes produced twenty bottles and in this year (1687) Skippe records that he gathered all the 'hard' grapes on 10 November, rather than in October, as in previous years, and this produced seven gallons of wine — perhaps 'ice-wine'. Of course, it is possible that some of the fruit used in the winemaking may have been grown outside the walled garden but the quantities involved could easily have been harvested from a few rows of soft fruit planted on the steeper slopes at the top of the enclosure. We know from the list discussed above that at least two vines could be found on the walls of the garden but the quantities involved make it more likely that the Vineyard at Wall Hills was the source. However, it is likely that this name predated the Skippe ownership of the place and relates to the well-documented winemaking activities of the bishop of Hereford in the 13th century.[21]

It is fitting that we should take our leave of George Skippe sitting in his summerhouse 'betwixt 9-10 in the forenoon', reading, perhaps, John Worlidge's *Vinetum Britannicum* (1676), which was later to be found in his library. No doubt he had a cup of his latest vintage in his hands and beneath his feet were neat rows of currants and gooseberries. On the walls at either side were well-trained fruit trees, all carefully labelled. Far below, close to the house, we may imagine his wife Elizabeth and the youngest of his seven children busy amongst the flowers and herbs planted in the *parterre à l' anglaise* among the box and yew hedges. Above them was the upstanding mansion with the adjoining spire of St. Peter's (now St. Michael's and All Angels), the parish church. In the distance through the blue haze we glimpse Marcle Hill ... *et in Arcadia ego*. George Skippe died in November 1690.

The summerhouse and the walled garden disappear from view during the 18th century but reappear to be admired by a 13-year-old boy, Edward Baker of Bayford, Hertfordshire, who wrote to his sister in *c*.1792: 'We rode to Mr. Skippe's which is situated just above the town of Ledbury. There is a nice paddock with deer there which we saw; the garden is a very good one, behind the house, and at the top of it is a summer house, from whence you cannot think what a beautiful view we saw'. The following day Edward enjoyed roast venison (presumably from the paddock), which was cooked on a turnspit, worked by a small dog in a wheel. 'After dinner it turned out fine, I and William went into Mr. Skippe's garden, at the top of which is a summer house from whence we saw an extensive view'.[22] The walled garden and its summerhouse are shown on an enclosure map of 1816 and again, on a smaller scale, on a *Map of Ledbury and its Environs* (1831) by E.W. Gibbs.[23] The Tithe Map of 1841 is more informative, showing the majority of the garden as a series of cultivated plots with an area of lawn along its lowest (eastern) extremity where two buildings at each corner are marked. On the north and west there are wall-side beds bounded by a perimeter path with the summerhouse at the apex. Near the bottom, adjacent to the north wall, is a narrow detached structure, perhaps a pavilion, and behind it, a small slip garden outside the wall, where on later maps there was a pump. On the south side of the garden, below the retaining wall there is another large building, perhaps a glasshouse.

An estate plan of 1843, drawn by Robert Jones, a Ledbury surveyor, which is displayed in the entrance hall of Upper Hall, adds further significant detail (Plate II). The mechanical and random treatment of the garden plots revealed on the Tithe Map are shown here as a geometric plan with the compartments focussing upon a circular garden (or lawn) occupying the upper or western end of the enclosure. Surprisingly, this feature must have been accommodated on the steep slope, for there is no sign of a level platform here today. Surrounding the circle are planting areas of different size and character, each one shaded to suggest a different regime. The buildings represented on the Tithe Map are all reproduced in the same position. Unfortunately, we have no way of telling if this plan reflects a modified original or 19th-century revivalist design but certainly there is no hint here of the picturesque or garden-esque tendencies of the early 19th century.

In 1812 Upper Hall was inherited by John Martin, MP for Tewkesbury, from his mother Penelope Skippe. The house was leased to the Revd. Reginald Pyndar, whose widow was still resident in 1835. It was left to John Martin II (d.1880) to acknowledge the fine qualities of the place by living there. He improved the parkland setting by planting many exotic trees and towards the end of his life was employing fifteen

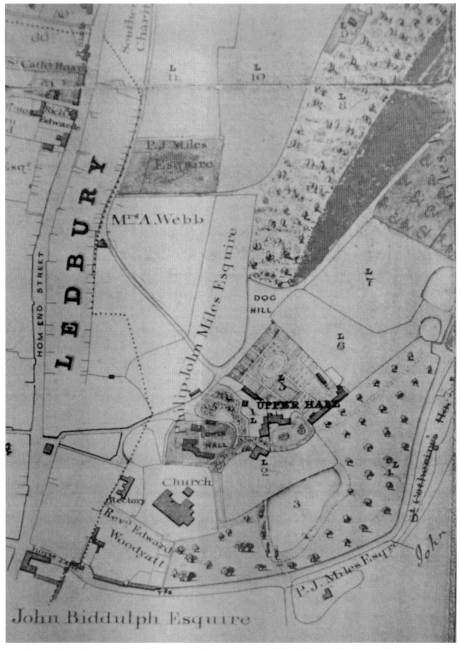

Plate II.   Estate plan drawn by Robert Jones (1843) — the formal design of the garden is revealed here

gardeners.[24] The old walled garden itself was given a makeover which perfectly reflects the eclectic tastes of the late 19th century. This is revealed on the first large scale OS plan of 1887 and more specifically, the later edition of this employed to accompany a sale catalogue of 1919 (Plate III).[25] Here the rustic formality which was still evident in the 1840s has given way to something much more self-conscious, embracing both the picturesque as well as the Old English style. The eastern end of the garden has been thrown open to the park. The wall and presumably the entrance gate have been removed and replaced with a broad walk 'lined with clipped (fastigiated) yews of striking uniformity'. Above this was an 'old established topiary and rose garden' which focussed upon a 'garden house' (first revealed upon the Tithe Map) at its northern extremity. In 1887 there was a small greenhouse/conservatory here but this had been removed by 1919 (Figs. 6 & 7). Indeed, comparing the two maps it is clear that the 'old' topiary garden was a piece of spurious antiquity and could easily have come from the contemporary works of J.D. Sedding, Reginald Blomfield or Inigo Triggs. The illustration in the sales catalogue shows small but elaborate tiered topiary with roses contained within low box hedges. It was certainly in the spirit of the age of George Skippe but he would have spurned the rather fragile and tinsel effect.

Fig. 6. The yew walk replacing the existing wall (Sale catalogue, 1919)

Equally contrived was the landscape above this where the earlier formality had been abandoned for serpentine paths winding their way through manicured lawns, punctuated with specimen trees. A Cedar of Lebanon and a 'fine Tulip tree' are noticed in the sale catalogue. We are

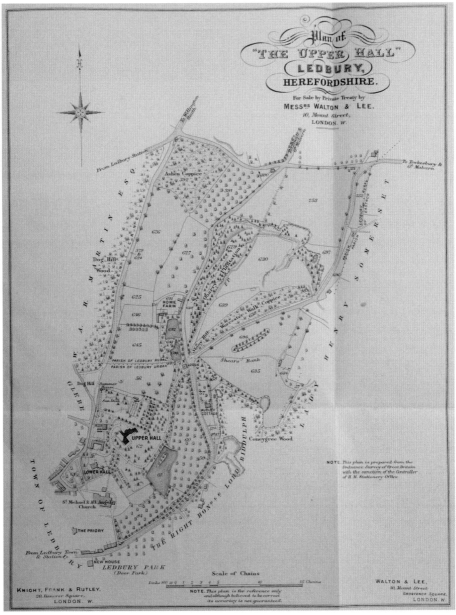

Plate III. The walled garden and its immediate surroundings
as shown on the 25 inch OS plan accompanying the sale catalogue of 1919

Fig. 7. 'The old established topiary and rose garden' (Sale catalogue, 1919)

told the walls here were lined with figs and on the way to the 'Queen Anne summerhouse' there was a sundial. The former was 'built of brick with slated roof, comprising an Open Summer House below, with Tea House having fireplace above ... enjoying extensive and charming panoramic views'. The illustration shows the summerhouse approached by a curving gravel path, surrounded by lawns with an island bed in the foreground (Fig. 8). On the southern side of the enclosure, below the retaining wall, there was a new kitchen garden (also apparent on an estate map of 1867) 'of about two-thirds of an acre in extent, well stocked with standard and wall fruit trees, and two other Fruit and Vegetable Gardens near the Glasshouses, (which) comprise Greenhouse and Peach House, Two Stove Houses, Melon and Cucumber House, and Vinery in two divisions, all heated; also a Ten light Brick Pit, Stoke Hole, Potting Shed, Fruit Room etc'.[26] Above this complex the yew-lined walk on the eastern side of the garden continued on a rising terrace until it met the west wall where there was an alcove seat.

After a spell as an auxiliary hospital during the First World War, Upper Hall and its 1,500-acre estate were sold by the Martin family in 1919. The mansion and its pleasure grounds were purchased by Herefordshire

Fig. 8. The summer-house (Sale catalogue, 1919)

County Council and Ledbury Grammar School was opened here in 1923. Initially there were few alterations to the grounds but in 1938 four tennis courts were established at the eastern end of the garden on the site of the yew walks. The ground was apparently levelled for this purpose. The upper part of the walled garden appears to have remained intact and vestiges of the topiary garden are apparent on an air photograph of 1939. Similarly, a pre-Second World War Aerofilms postcard indicates that the ground immediately below the Skippe's summerhouse was still open lawn. The kitchen garden with its many greenhouses was also intact and cultivation was taking place on the sloping ground below the yew walk on the south side of the garden. This was to change in the early 1950s when a science block was built on the site and further classrooms arrived in 1965 on the sloping area above the retaining wall. When the school moved to purpose-built premises in 1991 the mansion-house was restored as apartments, the tennis courts developed as four dwellings, known as Cedar Court and the Garden House built on the site of the science block/19th-century kitchen garden.[27]

Today, in terms of the general configuration of the landscape, little has changed since the late 19th century when the eastern end of the walled enclosure was demolished. There was never a wall on the south side looking down to the house. Today the lower yew walk still exists below Cedar Court, which sits on the footprint of the tennis courts.

*Plate IV. The fastigate yews on the southern boundary of the walled garden.
The wall shown here encloses the modern development (2007)*

The topiary garden above, albeit intact in 1919, presumably grew out of shape quickly with the removal of the fifteen gardeners employed by the Martins. The wall of the garden house/greenhouse noticed in the 1840s and later the focus of the topiary garden, still stands, redeveloped as a gazebo, in the garden of one of the new properties in Cedar Court. The fastigiate yews turn the south-eastern corner and continue to march along the southern boundary of the garden, thus perpetuating the original relationship between house and garden that existed in Skippe's time (Plate IV). The yews go further, passing the multi-stemmed Tulip Tree (*Liriodendron tulipifera*) that once overlooked the topiary garden, and come to a halt where in the late 19th-century beds were created above the 19th century kitchen garden. The terrace walk continues through the undergrowth to the west wall where it terminates in the ruined alcove with a semi-circular head moulded in the brickwork. From here, climbing the steep slope to Dog Hill the wall is complete and, similarly, from the site of the summerhouse down the north side of the garden to Cedar Court. The wall is almost ten feet high and capped with thick clay tiles, some of which have been dislodged by the encroaching ivy. The bricks are muddy-red in colour, typical of fabric derived from Old Red Sandstone clays. The dimensions of the bricks are variable but a typical example

Plate V. The steps up to the summerhouse at the top of the north wall (2007)

is 8½ long by 2⅛ inches thick. This is close to the Statute Brick of the Tudor period but smaller than the bricks used in London after the Restoration.[28] The bonding is also irregular but with headers very much in evidence. There are many smith-made diamond-headed nails on the inside of the wall but a fairly superficial search produced no lead tags naming the wall fruit.

The site of Skippe's summerhouse is marked by stone steps attached to the north wall and an associated lump of masonry, which appears to be the remains of one of the ground-floor arcades (Plate V). Much of the garden wall here has recently been repaired. Nearby is the damaged wrought iron ornamental rail from the steps with, rather characteristically, slender twisted barley-sugar balusters, so typical of the late 17th century. The summerhouse stands on a fairly spacious platform and with the eye of faith, it is just about possible to work out the route of the approaching path. There is much cotoneaster on the adjoining slopes, which has probably spread from the wall beds. The mature vegetation includes two cedars (*Cedrus libani*) and a Blue Atlas Cedar (*Cedrus atlantica 'glauca'*) — the latter nearer the summerhouse. There is also a large Holm Oak (*Quercus ilex*) close to the alcove on the terrace walk and, elsewhere, a Douglas Fir (*Pseudotsuga menziesii*) and, planted more recently, a number of Scots Pine (*Pinus sylvestris*) and European Larch

(*Larix deciduas*). Similarly, recently introduced are a few Common Beech (*Fagus sylvatica*) and a Copper Beech (*f. purpurea*) and there is much self generated Sycamore with an under-storey of young yews, Field Maple (*Acer campestre*), privet, Oregon Grape (*Mahonia aquifolium*), Cherry Laurel and *Cotoneaster atropurpureus*. The last four are clearly shrubs that have migrated from the late 19th-century borders. George Skippe's garden is certainly lost, but by no stretch of the imagination has it disappeared. Indeed, it turns out that this is one of those fortunate pieces of garden history where documents, maps and the artefact itself complement each other perfectly.

The Walled Gardens at Old Sufton and Sufton Court, Mordiford

Mordiford is a small village three miles east of Hereford at the western-most point of the Woolhope Hills and close to the River Lugg where it joins the Wye. The two properties of Sufton Court and Old Sufton are both owned by the Hereford family who have been established at Mordiford since the 12th century.[1]

Garden and landscape history is always archaeological and archival, and is often dependent on oral history to add colour to the cartography. The process of deduction can be analogous to drawing an outline from distant mirrors. In the case of Sufton Court there are some certain dates: for an inheritance, a marriage, the birth of an heir, the completion of a house, and a visit by Humphrey Repton that resulted in the Sufton House Red Book of 1795. Beyond that, while there is archival material for the estate woodlands and tenanted farms at the Hereford Record Office, there is nothing for the gardens: no gardeners' notebooks, no diaries, no letters, no memoirs, no seed catalogues or planting lists, to name some basic sources. For the 20th century, there is the oral history provided by Major Hereford and an aerial photograph from the 1950s. Old Sufton's garden is largely undocumented. So, to be clear, in the absence of rich archives, what follows is a contextual assessment of the two walled gardens, achieved through fieldwork, maps and general history.

In this case study, garden history becomes a parable of the fate of walled gardens over the last 200 years. Built with confidence and care, 18th-century walled gardens produced vast quantities of vegetables, fruit and flowers for an intensive period of about one hundred and fifty years. After 1918 there was a sharp decline, which accelerated into abandon-ment after 1945. There were exceptions, but for the most part, walled gardens became car parks, pony paddocks, conifer nurseries, were used for housing development, or simply left to grow derelict. The end of the 20th century has seen a revival of interest both in the history and in the fate of these once intense spaces. There is renovation, funding for restoration, interest in reducing food miles by growing locally, and a commitment to think of ways in which these once cultivated acres can be productive again.

Old Sufton

So, let us start in 1781, when Sir James Hereford writes his will in favour of James Caldecott, his eldest sister's son. The nephew is fifteen years old. He knows he will inherit the estate if not the title. What was that inheritance? It was the medieval manor farm of Old Sufton, which had been in the Hereford family for five hundred odd years at this point (Fig. 1).

The mansion at Old Sufton, with its 16th-century timber-framed heart sits low down, in the manner of ancient houses, in a natural cleft, worn by water in a limestone outcrop of the Woolhope Hills (Plate I).[2] It looks westwards across a fertile landscape of meadows and ploughlands established on the alluvium laid down at the confluence of the rivers Lugg and Frome with the Wye, just below Mordiford. On all other sides the ground rises steeply with craggy outcrops, enhanced later by 19th-century quarrying. A small stream, now rather silted up, runs from a pool above the house and is culverted under the old farmyard, once filled with barns, hop-kilns and stables (Plate II).

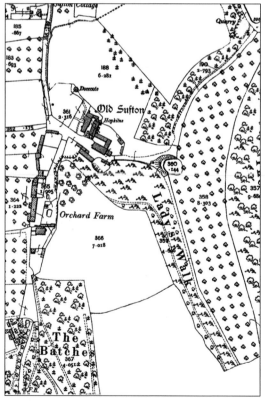

Fig. 1. 6 inch OS map of Old Sufton, 1883

The eastern frontage of the house looks out onto a flat

Plate I. General view of Old Sufton showing the mansion and the walled garden

lawned enclosure with low walls on the south and east. The entrance gate is now on the south, close to the house, but originally there was a path across the lawn to the west, which gave access to an ancient thoroughfare, running down to Mordiford Bridge. Before the establishment of a new turnpike road, closer to the flood plain in the late 18th century, this was one of the main roads of the Welsh border, bringing travellers from the south via Gloucester and Ledbury to Hereford and Wales.[3] It

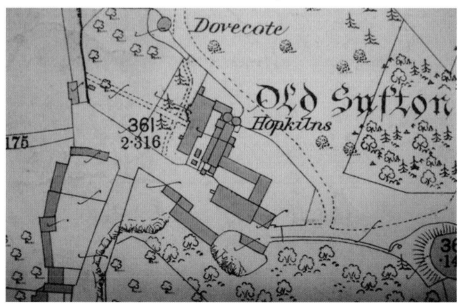

Plate II. 25 inch OS map of Old Sufton, 1883

33

Plate III. The garden wall and the summerhouse from the lawn

made Old Sufton appear much less withdrawn from the world than it seems today. The northern half of the garden enclosure rises dramatically to a high platform occupied by a circular dovecote, which is clasped by the garden wall that bravely mounts the steep gradient without any compromise. Albeit the wall remains low where the lawn is flat, it rises quickly to its full height of nine feet where it rises up the slope in the north-west corner of the garden (Plate III). Apart from an area close to the present gate, the brickwork throughout appears to be uniform and similar chevron-shaped capping stones are used on both the high and low wall. It probably dates from the late 18th century.

Seen from the outside the wall is much higher and more impressive than it appears internally, suggesting that a good deal of levelling has taken place within the garden. Quite close to the south gate it is apparent that the brick wall was built on rubble stone foundations, which increasingly dominate the external profile, and where the wall begins to rise up the gradient from the old road to Prior's Frome, its external face is entirely stone (Plate IV). The brick, two courses deep, is simply used on the internal face and on the top to protect the stonework from erosion. On the inside there are frequent brick buttresses bonded into the wall, many of them out of vertical (Plate V). A particularly impressive brick buttress is used externally to strengthen the high stone wall close to the lane.

Plate IV. The high wall from the exterior

Plate V. The internal brick buttresses

The wall to the east of the dovecote, running down to the north wing of the house, is around six feet high and clamped into the bank. It appears to be brick on the inside, stone outside, but obscured by a dense growth of ivy. The only break in the wall occurs to the west of the dovecote, where there is a low gate leading out onto the hillside to join the track running up from the low ground beyond the farmhouse. Adjoining the door, high in the wall, but close to the dovecote is a window blocked with the same late 18th-century brick-fabric used in the wall (Fig. 2).

This feature suggests that the exterior stone wall predates the interior brickwork and may relate to an earlier building built against the wall. The brick wall is two bricks in depth and laid in a mixed garden bond where no attempt is made to place the headers above each other (as in the Flemish bond) and the stretchers are laid in twos and threes. The bricks

Fig. 2. Dovecote and external wall showing the door and earlier window (NMR photograph taken in 1890 by Alfred Watkins — original in Hereford City Library (HCL), Pilley 351)

Plate VI. Two doors giving access to the pigeon loft and the summerhouse

are fairly large, $9^3/_8$ x $2^1/_2$ x $4^3/_8$ inches being typical, which suggests an 18th century date.[4] The texture is fairly coarse but the colour brighter than most Herefordshire fabric of this period, perhaps as a result of limestone in the clay. The lime-mortar in the joints is fairly pronounced and still holding fast although many of the capping tiles have disappeared and the pilaster buttresses also lack their covering.

The circular dovecote is certainly the outstanding feature of the walled garden with the walls abutting on either side, placed at the highest point in the garden. The usual diameter for circular dovecotes is between 15 and 16 feet but this one must be close to 20 and has similar properties to a large dovecote at Cowarne Court, which is 18 feet in diameter and originally had a stone vaulted roof, suggesting a medieval date.[5] Today the dovecote at Old Sufton is boarded-up and access impossible. The building is approached by a path from the house, which runs close to the inside of the north wall. Two sentinel yews stand guard where the path passes through a short cross wall from the house to the garden wall. On the east side of the dovecote, looking down the path, are two doors providing evidence for an additional function served by the building (Plate VI). One of the doors leads up to the pigeon loft, which Watkins noticed only occupied the top of the building. The other door gives access to the ground floor, where there is a room with a large window embracing a remarkable prospect towards the south and west. Thus, the Sufton dovecote was more than a utilitarian building; it acted as a summerhouse and until recently the internal walls were still dressed with patterned wallpaper.

Three phases of building can be detected in the fabric. The first phase is indicated in the rubble-stone wall, visible at the rear, where some of the original plaster rendering is still attached to the surface. The stone fabric may be present on the garden front but here the facing is brick, laid neatly in Flemish bond with thin lime-mortar courses. The wall meets the roof with a simple dentil frieze of end-on bricks. Above the doors are semi-circular recesses with a neat (but crumbling) voussoir over the window. The brickwork around the window is bulging and may be of a different period since there is a string-course here, which simply fades away on the south-east side of the building. Originally the roof supported a glazed octagon lantern with a flamboyant weathervane above displaying a double-headed eagle, the initials IHM and the date 1764 (see Fig. 2). These clearly belong to Sir James and Martha Hereford (I being the Latin initial for James) who were presumably responsible for the brick embellishments to the summerhouse and the walled garden. This was twenty-five years before the next generation of Herefords left Old Sufton for Sufton (Place) Court on the adjoining hill.

The summerhouse/dovecote now sits in a wilderness of brambles and rough grass. A large multi-stemmed yew — perhaps formerly topiarised — stands just below the building where thirty years ago it was still possible to trace the lines of box hedging accompanying the paths. In the Spring naturalised daffodils flower on the slopes and there is still much wild marjoram (*Origanum vulgare*), which on a warm September day, when this survey took place, attracted Red Admiral and Comma butterflies. The marjoram, we might speculate, derived from a long-lost herb garden but probably not, as wild marjoram likes limestone, which underpins this garden. There are many nail holes on the walls from long-lost fruit and no doubt the labels could be recovered from the foot of the wall if cultivation was ever to take place again. In its 18th-century heyday this was probably an 'old-fashioned' garden where fruit, vegetables and flowers were organised in formal compartments with the flowers and vegetables on the flat area near the house whilst the fruit trees and bushes occupied the steep slopes, accessed by box-lined zigzag paths. This was similar to George Skippe's garden at Upper Hall, Ledbury where gooseberries and currents were planted on the steep ascent to the summerhouse on the apex of a hill — all very reminiscent of Old Sufton.

The suggestion that the walled enclosure and summerhouse/dovecote at Old Sufton had an earlier life before Sir James refurbished it in 1764 raises the tantalising question of its earlier provenance and the possibility that this exceptional site played a part in John Evelyn's model for a British Elysium at Backbury. This had been suggested to him by a local correspondent, John Beale, the author of *Herefordshire Orchards: A Pattern for all England* (1657), who was very familiar with the area around Old Sufton, having taken refuge in the crevices of Backbury Hill during the early years of the English Civil War, where he communicated with God and Nature and experienced a Pauline encounter. Furthermore, Beale was familiar with members of the Hereford family: with Henry Hereford 'the mystic', a fellow of St. John's, Oxford and his sister Jane, who, according to a note in the Mordiford Parish Register, later became Beale's wife. This celebrated landscape, the precocious forerunner of the English landscape garden, has been much discussed, most recently by Peter Goodchild.[6] It was an extensive area, which embraced a quadrant of varied land with Backbury Hill at its apex. At the foot of the hill, according to Beale, there stood a mansion, where 'a rich pure fountain' passed to one side and adjoining it was a 'garden plot upon a Rock' which was 'perpetually verdant and could be extended to embrace more of the hillside' and was eminently suitable for the planting of 'Medicinal Simples (herbs), Vinyards etc'. The description fits perfectly the situation of the walled garden. The summerhouse upon the rock may have appeared as one of the 'artificial accomplishments' Evelyn speculated could be added to the site to make it 'one of the most august and magnificent gardens in the world, so far exceeding those of Italy and France'. The dreams of 'Elysium Britannicum' were, to some extent, fulfilled by Sir James Hereford in 1764 when he remodelled the summerhouse from whence he could sit, as John Beale had presumably done before him, and admire the 'rich vales of ravishing varieties' in the landscape at his feet.

Sufton Court

James Hereford inherited Old Sufton at the age of 20, in 1786. A year later he married the daughter of a Commodore Mendes. Her portrait in Sufton Court shows a well-presented, smart, pretty young woman. They were a young couple with the unusual situation of being in control of a property upon majority rather than middle age. A little over a year after marriage, a son and heir is born in 1789. At this point, James Hereford was Mayor of Hereford and living in the city, a position indicative of both his local standing and his ambition. As a prominent couple of substance, they desired a house to reflect that position and incorporate contemporary ideas of convenience, light and situation. By 1790, they were living in one, called Sufton Place and later Court, on a rise above Mordiford village, and roughly half a mile south of Old Sufton (Plate VII).

Two architects have been cited as involved in the design of Sufton Court: Anthony Keck and James Wyatt. Anthony Keck is suggested because of nearby Longworth Hall and the similarities with Canon Frome Court and Moccas Court, which he also designed. The common feature appears to be the tripartite Venetian window, which they all share.[7] James Wyatt is cited by W.H. Cooke, an antiquarian who lived at Sufton Court in the late 19th century. Wyatt was working in Hereford in 1788, when James Hereford was Mayor, and at the time, 'was acknowledged as the most fashionable architect of his day.'[8] Sufton Court is not included in Wyatt's list of houses but it seems likely that the two

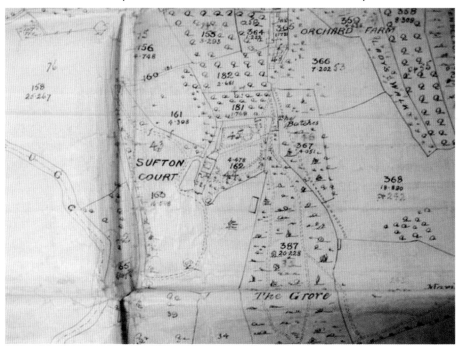

Plate VII. Estate notations over the 1883 map

Plate VIII James Wathen's sketch, 13 March 1790

men would have met in the course of business associated with Hereford Cathedral although Wyatt did not get involved here until the summer of 1788.[9] Whoever did it, the house was in use, with a walled kitchen garden in place by the time that Humphrey Repton came to visit five years later on two rainy days of 27 and 28 April 1795.

Sufton Court was built to be seen from the bridge over the Lugg at Mordiford. Ancillary stables lie below the dip, so the house appears unencumbered and pristine. The walled garden sits behind and to the north side of the house, where it catches the sun but is out of sight. It has four quarters and a central water source. Beyond it, to the north, there were orchards, according to Repton's sketch of 1795. A watercolour by James Wathen gives a sense of the newly completed Sufton Court on 'Friday at 12.00 13 March 1790'[10] (Plate VIII).

In April 1795, Humphrey Repton came for two days and he delivered his Red Book in July of the same year.[11] Sufton is one of six properties he worked on in Herefordshire and he used the Sufton site as part of his polemic with Richard Payne Knight and Uvedale Price, 'My opinion concerning the improvement of Sufton Court involves so many points, which I deem principles in the art of Landscape Gardening that I trust you will permit one to take this opportunity of justifying my practice, in opposition to the wild theory of improvements which has lately sprung up in Herefordshire.' In fact, he made a professional virtue out of his short visit by eschewing the process of imbibing the supposed atmosphere of the place in a quasi-picturesque way. Instead, he offered a modern service, delineating clear approach lines, panoramic views, practical notes on internal use in order to get the best of the external

41

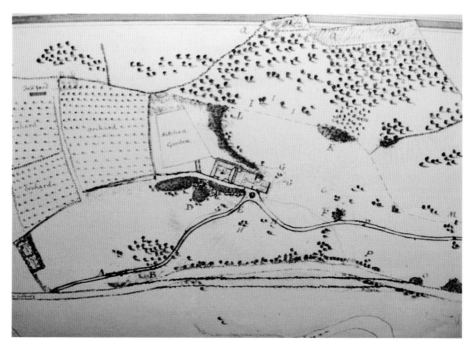

Plate IX. Repton's sketch-map of 1795 showing the relationship between the house, services and the kitchen garden

views, and unsentimental logistics. His sketch map of Sufton Court is very helpful in showing the kitchen garden (Plate IX).

The Red Book itself is rather anodyne, with a series of undeveloped and similar views. A few hedges are taken out, a few clumps are planted and the larger landscape to the west, over the meadows, is incorporated into the view from the house. Nothing is mentioned of the walled garden. It was probably laid out according to conventional purposes and design and was already in production.

What is noticeable from maps is that a circuit walk was designed to link Old Sufton and Sufton Court. It circuits southwards from Old Sufton through Ladies Walk, and across to the Batches. A longer walk goes through the Pendlehopes copse, around the Shrubberies, behind a clump of trees, and up to the eastern entrance of Sufton Court (Plate X).

Repton's influence can be seen in the small arboretum to the south of the walled garden, a pleasing approach to the domestic entrance at the close of the circuit. When, how and why is unknown at this point, but the walk is still a discernible contour through Ladies Walk, and obvious

42

on the longer terrace of the Pendlehopes and Shrubberies while a few ornamental shrubs remain in the shrubberies. It could be that the rampart wall and dovecote became an eye-catcher on the hill above Old Sufton and the sheltered pleasaunce in front became a destination for female pedestrians (Plate XI).

To return to the walled garden, it is possible to construct from family oral history and maps what the basic elements were of the walled garden for the next 120 years. There was a vine house. The quarter plots were edged with low, espalier apple trees. There was an apple store, a greenhouse, and

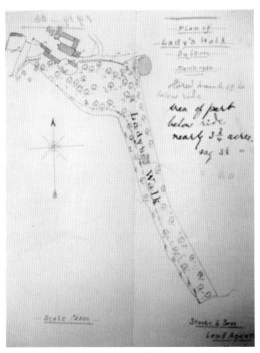

Plate X. Annotated 19th-century map showing the Lady's Walk to Old Sufton

a coke stove to heat it. Up to the mid 1920s, the walled garden remained in full production, but by the end of the 1930s, although the structures

Plate XI. An early 19th-century chalk sketch showing the juvenile planting in the park at Sufton Court

remained, there was only one gardener, and activity was consequently reduced (Fig. 3).

In the 1960s, the structures began to fall to pieces, and in the early 1970s, the buildings and three walls were taken down and the rubble used to build tracks on the estate. The south-facing wall is all that remains, and the acre of ground was incorporated into the

43

adjacent field, which had once been an orchard. In the early 1990s, the Herefords reinstated the north-facing boundary with a hornbeam hedge. Old Sufton was a tenanted farm until the 1920s, at which point the last tenant retired and the house became a residence until the late 1950s. It remained empty until the 1980s and is now tenanted

Fig. 3. Kitchen garden in 1949
(Major and Mrs. James Hereford)

again. Old Sufton never caught the eye of an early 20th-century manor house enthusiast as did Sutton Courtenay and Avebury.[12]

Sufton Court's walled garden illustrates the rise and fall and potential rise of many walled gardens. Walled gardens are pivotal episodes in the landscape of a house such as Sufton Court. The domestic order is extended into nature and nature is ordered into productive and edible artifice. The second half of the 20th century saw decline of this social and vegetative hierarchy. What remains at Sufton Court is an outline. Without documentation, one is shaping a broad outline of a story.

In other words, Sufton Court's walled garden is a parable. It is worth recording as a memory but there is, at present, little else beyond the one remaining wall to indicate that once there was a bustling, productive space with colour, scent, design, and achievement packed into one acre. The empty field plot that is now being recalled with a boundary re-instatement waits for resurrection in a new form, in some future decade, whilst a few hundred yards away at Old Sufton one of the most significant walled gardens in the region also awaits restoration.

Afterword
Subsequent to the writing of this account in 2007, the dovecote/summer-house at Old Sufton has been fully restored. Bravo!

Downton Castle and its Walled Garden

Richard Payne Knight (1750-1824) inherited the Downton estate in 1772 from his grandfather, Richard Knight (1659-1745), an ironmaster with business interests in south Shropshire, Worcestershire and Herefordshire. Richard Payne then commenced building Downton Castle, created a garden around it, with an unusual, irregular octagonal walled garden to the north (Fig.1) and laid out a landscape park in the estate in accordance with his views expressed in 1794 in a long didactic poem entitled *The Landscape*.[1] In 1809 Downton Castle was handed over to Richard

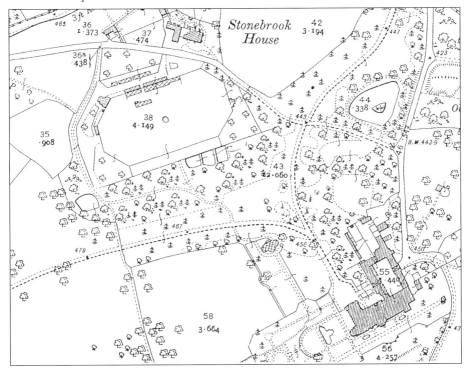

Fig. 1. 2nd edition OS map, 1903

Payne's brother, Thomas Andrew (1759-1838), who put his own mark on the garden. Richard Payne and Thomas Andrew were the sons of the Revd. Thomas Knight and Ursula (née Nash) of Wormsley Grange, Herefordshire, and were born into a talented family, including a cousin, Col. Thomas Johnes (1748-1816) of Croft Castle and Hafod,[2] who was a translator of French literature and printer of fine books, and had similar tastes to Richard Payne.

Thomas Andrew had lived at Elton Hall, Herefordshire, not far from Downton Castle, after his marriage in 1791, and had developed his interest and expertise in scientific horticulture in the garden at Elton. The picturesque ideas of Richard Payne for gardening and landscaping were in complete contrast to the thoughts of his brother. In 1809 when he moved to Downton Castle, Thomas Andrew took with him his approach to using a garden as a laboratory, and by then he was acknowledged as a leading horticultural scientist; he became, from 1811, the second President of the (Royal) Horticultural Society of London.[3] For Thomas Andrew gardening at Downton Castle became experimental horticulture, with the walled kitchen garden one of the sites for his experiments.

Evidence of how Thomas Andrew used the grounds is given in a comment in 1838 by an observer writing in the *Gardener's Magazine*:

> Except a narrow lawn, planted with a few shrubs, there are no ornamental grounds, attached to the castle, Mr. Knight being of the opinion that such decorative accompaniments would be out of character with its simple grandeur ...[4]

Knight did not entirely ignore aesthetics and ornamental plants, as two papers on cultivation of the Guernsey Lily and one on Cockscomb were presented to the Horticultural Society of London.

A description of the kitchen garden in Thomas Andrew's time was also given in 1838 in the *Gardener's Magazine*:

> The kitchen-garden is the principal seat of Mr. Knight's horticultural experiments. It stands a few hundred yards northward of the house, on the side of a bank which falls gently to the south. Its area is not large, and it is, besides, greatly encumbered by large seedling fruit trees, the result of Mr. Knight's hybridisations, which, consequently, cannot be removed until the value of their produce has been ascertained. The hot-houses also are not connected in a range with a view to effect, but are widely scattered over the ground ...

Knight indicates in his correspondence and papers how experiments were set up; one entry for August 1798 from his garden notebook [5] shows his use of the garden with his setting up hybridisations of peas at Elton, and this approach continued at Downton Castle:

Peas sown in front of the vinery
↑N
points of the pods to the west
1 Row of pods of gray rouncival
impregnated by white frame pea.
2 Row of pods of best new variety
impreg[d] by a minute quantity
of pollen of gray rouncival.
3 Row ditto of pods on same
stem, but the quantity of pollen
not quite so small.
4 ...

Experiments with peas were carried out as Thomas Andrew wished to obtain results of cross-pollinations more quickly than could be achieved from his fruit breeding. The results of fruit breeding experiments with apples and pears cannot be obtained for about a decade from the cross-pollinations, hence the comment about the kitchen garden at Downton Castle being 'encumbered by large seedling fruit trees'.

Plate I. Curvilinear greenhouse in the walled kitchen garden

Plate II. Detail of glass and iron framework

The garden changed over the years with the different interests of subsequent occupants of Downton Castle, and very little remans today in the walled garden of Thomas Andrew's experimental garden. Indeed a record in 1998 by Dr. Paul Stamper[6] shows that features such as a tennis court had been subsequently laid out. The fabric of a curvilinear greenhouse with an iron framework survives (Plate I), including some of the fine shaped glass, and is now a grade II listed building of special architectural or historic interest (Plate II). The framework of iron is a reminder of the source of the family wealth from Coalbrookdale. According to an anonymous publication of 1822 about pineapples, possibly written by J.C. Loudon,[7] this structure was purchased in June 1820 from Messrs W. and D. Bailey of London. There were originally several glasshouses of different types and these were erected over several years. For instance, one earlier record in a letter from Thomas Andrew to Sir Joseph Banks in October 1819[8] states that a hothouse was 'not built till the end of May'.

The curvilinear glasshouse was purchased to enable Thomas Andrew to conduct investigations on the growth of cultivated plants at a time of interest in determining the best environmental conditions for growing plants under glass, including the angle of the glass to the sun. The curvilinear design arose out of an interaction of ideas which started with the publication in 1803 of a treatise by Anderson[9] on a patent hot-house and a paper by Knight in 1805[10] in which he considered the general issues needing the attention of the newly formed (Royal) Horticultural Society of London. Later, in 1808, Knight[11] discussed greenhouse design and

48

concluded that an angle of 34 degrees was best for the glass. In 1815 the issue was taken up with G.S. Mackenzie[12] who then advocated a curvilinear structure, and Knight[13] agreed with this proposition in a paper published in 1817. The earliest published reference by Thomas Andrew to the cultivation of plants in his curvilinear greenhouse with an iron framework was in 1822[14] in a paper called 'Upon the Culture of the Pine apple, without bark, or other Hot Bed' in the *Transactions of Horticultural Society of London.*

The pineapple was a matter of considerable interest as it was something of a status symbol and as an introduced plant required much care to achieve results. Thomas Andrew first started growing pineapples at Downton Castle in 1817 when he received nine plants. His preoccupation was the maintenance of a high temperature whilst at the same time ensuring a turnover of air. Knight used structures in his kitchen garden for investigations in growing pineapples in ordinary and stove conditions and in 1828[15] reported that, having 'sacrificed many plants in experiments', he found that stove dry conditions were not suitable and likewise very low temperatures retarded growth. The cultural method used at Downton Castle was omission of bottom heat and a bark bed, and this seemingly had no ill-effects. Knight propagated pineapples by a different method to that adopted by others as he used suckers broken off when they were four or five inches long. Thomas Andrew obviously succeeded in growing pineapples at Downton Castle as Joseph Sabine, in a footnote to Knight's paper published in 1830,[16] testified to the quality of the fruit as being 'universally destitute of fibre'.

Knight's interest in curvilinear structures led him to send to the Horticultural Society of London in September 1822 a paper on 'curvilinear iron roofs to hot houses'. In October 1822 the Council of the Horticultural Society of London considered purchasing a curvilinear greenhouse to grow tropical fruits at its Chiswick gardens and agreed to obtain plans for one.[17]

The anonymous pamphlet on the cultivation of pineapples published in 1822[18] gave credit to Knight in the title. Loudon, if he was the author, changed his opinion by 1827 when there was controversy with both Knight and the Horticultural Society of London in *The Gardener's Magazine,* of which Loudon was the editor. The Council responded in 1828 by returning the offending issue of *The Gardener's Magazine*, and afterwards a partial apology was published. Knight continued to grow pineapples at Downton Castle with success and reprints of his papers were published and reprinted at home and abroad. However, ironically, despite his success, by 1838[19] Knight had stopped growing pineapples because 'they were not generally liked by those who dined at his table'.

The landscaped parkland around Downton Castle created by Richard Payne was also used for experiments by his brother. For example, trees were being used by Thomas Andrew for investigations into the flow of sap when the French scientist Monsieur Henri Dutrochet of Tours visited Downton Castle during 1827, as he reported in 1832 to Professor Augustin Pyramus de Candolle of Geneva:[20]

> During a visit which he paid me here, I had the alburnum of an oak tree cut through in his presence, and the leaves all immediately faded and died.

The parkland around Downton Castle still retains the style envisaged by Richard Payne and is a legacy of his thinking about the picturesque landscape (Plate III); and his brother's work also lives on, not so much in the physical garden itself as in the results and influence of his work there, which became a testimony to his belief in the importance of scientific horticulture, which led to the shaping of an institution whose work continues today: as a founder of the Horticultural Society of London[21], Thomas Andrew Knight had a vision when drafting a prospectus for the new society in 1805[22] that it should be for advancement of a scientific approach to understanding the growth of cultivated plants.

Plate III. Downton Castle and its landscape setting above the River Teme

The Walled Garden at Nieuport House, Almeley

Every now and again one comes across the story of a walled garden with a happy ending. Even after years of abandonment and neglect, a garden may yet be rescued and restored back to productive life. The one at Nieuport House, Almeley is such a garden, the new owners having embarked on a radical programme of restoration of the 18th-century walled garden.

The story begins in 1712, when Thomas, first Lord Foley of Great Witley, an ironmaster, purchased the Nieuport estate from the Pember family. He then demolished the medieval house and built the present house sometime between 1712 and 1718. The central block of the house is made up of seven bays, with two storey, two bay pavilions on either side. There are now two projecting stone bays at the front which were added later in the 19th century. The architect is unknown.

The painting *The Stag Hunt at Newport, c.*1718 (Plate I), shows the new house surrounded by a formal garden, with two main walled areas, one directly in front of the house with terraced walks on three sides and a 'sunken octagonal basin' in the centre. The other to the west is, we can assume, at least in part productive, with fruit trees and vegetables grown for the table. A triangular fishpond lies to the front of the gardens, and in the foreground is the curved park boundary wall. From what we make out from this painting, which now sadly exists only as a photograph, this appears to be a typical layout of a formal garden of the 17th and early 18th centuries, with the ornamental garden laid out to the front of the house and the productive garden set to one side.

Thomas Foley of Stoke Edith had set up his grandson, Paul Foley, at Nieuport shortly after the purchase, and it is his letters and accounts, relating to estate matters, that form a substantial archive housed in

Plate I. The Stag Hunt at Nieuport, c.1718 (Mr. A.T. Foley).

the Hereford Record Office. In letters written to his bailliff, Paul Foley
expresses a keen interest in his garden and in his fruit trees in particular,
for on 23 October 1731 he writes 'there is part of an apple tree hangs
over the wall in the kitchen garden, so much as hangs over I would have
cut down for it destroys the Wall fruit tree. There is a good peach tree
at the end of the partridge house in the Long Walk. I would have it
removed and put in the room of the tree dead in the south wall of the
Kitchen Garden ...'[1] The following year Foley obtains new trees from a
local nurseryman, 'as to the tree you want for the garden get it off the
nursery man at Shobden and when you tell him the aspect of the wall
what wind it stands to he will tell you what tree is most proper', relying
on his expertise to advise on the appropriate variety.[2] This nurseryman is
most likely to be Thomas Greening of nearby Shobdon Court, gardener
to George II.[3]

The grounds at Nieuport, in common with most other country estates
at this time, underwent radical change later in the century. In line with
current fashionable theories on landscape design, the formal gardens
were removed and replaced by a more 'natural' design. Figure 1 is based
on a beautiful hand-painted and coloured map of 1767, describing
the intended improvements suggested by John Bach, a Herefordshire
schoolmaster turned landscape designer.[4] The plan shows that the
formal walled gardens have disappeared and in their place is a semicir-

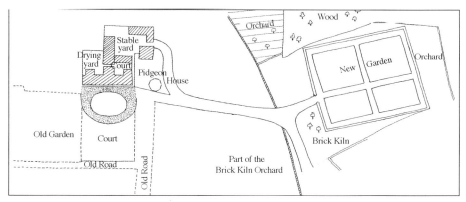

Fig. 1. John Bach's 1767 plan

cular gravel turning circle around an oval lawn, the main approach to the house has been altered and the new kitchen garden is sited approximately 200 metres from the house to the east. Not all the proposed changes appear to have taken place, but the kitchen garden, described in the map and other correspondence as the New Garden, is in its present position, albeit larger than is shown on this plan.

The re-siting of the New Garden at some distance from the house certainly reflects the aesthetic preoccupations of the period.[5] But there were also more pragmatic reasons for this relocation. New varieties of fruit trees from the continent, particularly apricot, peaches and nectarines, required higher walls as 'these could not be adequately dwarfed'.[6] A wider variety of vegetables was becoming increasingly available and a growing understanding of their special requirements led to an acceptance that a specially designated area was required. There is plenty of evidence to date the building of the New Garden precisely, with many accounts and invoices referring to building the new walls, such as one from June 1768 which reads 'Paid Thomas Savage 6½ days @10d sinking the foundation for the new garden wall and cutting a drain' and even 'drawing nails from the old walls 5/5d',[7] demonstrating that recycling is not exclusively a 21st century preoccupation. The bricks from the old garden were also recycled, as described in an invoice the following month for 'taking down the old garden walls & cleaning 31 thousand of Brick at 20d P. thous'.[8] This process must have been replicated throughout the country.

A fascinating reference to a payment 'for 5 baggs of scraps of cloth to nail the wall trees 2/6d'[9] suggests a possible cottage industry for strips of washed cloth, ready to be used for tying and nailing the fruit trees against the wall. There are many other similar references, and this method was the norm until the more general use of wire stretchers from around the mid 19th century.

A later estate plan of 1774 (Fig. 2) shows the completed improve-ments. The New Garden is in the same position but has been extended laterally and the layout of the paths follows a more symmetrical arrangement.[10] By my rough calculations it appears to be its present size of around 120 metres long and 60 metres wide, approximately 0.8 hectares. However it is noticeably skewed towards the south-east which is in keeping with early 18th-century

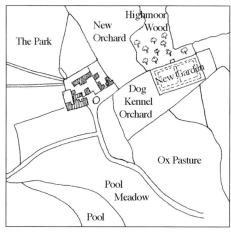

Fig. 2. Estate plan, 1774

thinking on the positioning of walled gardens. In *The Practical Fruit Gardener being the best and newest method of raising, planting and pruning all sorts of fruit-trees* (first published in 1724) Stephen Switzer wrote that 'in my opinion, a south wall, inclining about 20° to the east, is preferable to any other, inasmuch as the sun shines as early on it as a full east wall and never departs from it til about 2 o'clock in the afternoon'.[11] The idea was that the important south wall was exposed to the sun as early as possible, and although it would lose the sun earlier, the bricks would retain the heat for some time after the sun had moved on. However, by my rough calculations, the wall is nearer 35° to the east, almost twice as much as that advocated by Switzer, perhaps because by the time the garden was built, Thomas Hitt had published his theories of wall orien-tation in his *Treatise on Fruit-Trees* in 1755. Hitt suggested orienting the garden at a 45° angle, which he believed would create the optimum temperatures for the carefully selected varieties of fruit trees trained on the appropriate walls.[12]

The walls are mostly brick but part of the northern side of the north wall is faced with stone, so this was clearly not intended as a fruit wall. To the north-west the garden is sheltered by Highmoor Wood, and centrally placed, in prime position in the north wall, is the small gardener's cottage, built at the same time as the garden.

By the 1770s the Hon. Andrew Foley, Paul Foley's son, was master at Nieuport, and 'added much to its beauties, by extending walks and plantations'.[13] Nieuport estate remained in the ownership of the Foley family until 1863 when it was sold to James Watt Gibson-Watt, grandson of the Scottish engineer James Watt. Only ten years later, however, it was sold on to a Mrs. Gurney Pease.[14] She did not reside there, and the house and gardens were let to a series of tenants.[15] One imagines that the garden continued to be cultivated and retained its traditional quadripartite layout as can be seen in the first edition OS map of 1891 (Fig. 3). The map shows that glass had been introduced along the south side of the north wall at some point in the century: most likely a range of vineries. The Gardener's Cottage is in the same position as on the 1774 plan, on an axis with the cross path which ends in a gate in the south wall. The longer cross path leads to another entrance centrally placed in the west wall, possibly for the use of the family, although it has been recently discovered during restoration work that this was a later, probably 19th century, addition.

By 1904 there was a much greater range of glass as shown in the 2nd edition OS map of that year. In the Sales Particulars of 1909 these are described as a 'lean-to Cucumber House, Forcing House, Vinery and

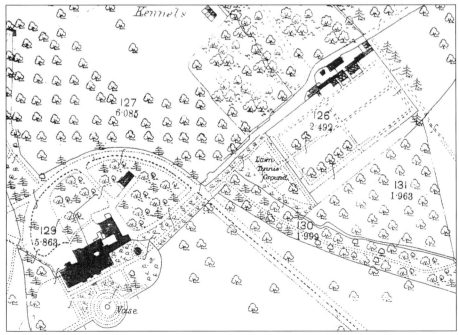

Fig. 3. OS map, 1891

55

Fernery, the whole being heated by a newly installed "Robin Hood" boiler'.[16] Unfortunately none of this glass survives although the footings are still in evidence. The only remaining glasshouse is a Foster and Pearson full span house, extending lengthways from the wall as shown in the 1928 OS edition (Fig. 4). This must have been erected sometime between 1904 and 1909; a Foster and Pearson catalogue of 1909 cites the purchaser as Mr. de Cliffe

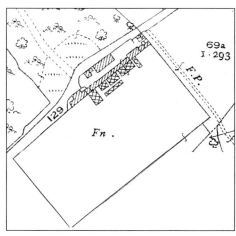

Fig. 4. OS map, 1928

Vigors,[17] possibly the son of the Revd. Richard Vigors, who was a tenant there for nine years. The glasshouse would have been heated (but the pipes have since been removed) and probably used as a general purpose 'plant house' for growing orchids and other exotics for the house.

The 1909 sales particulars describes the garden at the time as being an 'excellent Walled Fruit and Vegetable garden of upwards of Two Acres, well stocked with Standard, Espalier and Wall fruit trees' and goes on to describe the range of outbuildings as:

> Consisting of Stoke-Hole, Coal Shed, Men's Water Closet, Store Room, Apple Room, Bothy, Office, Potting Shed, Mushroom House and Boiler House, two sets of double Piggeries with yards, Manure Pits and a timber and corrugated iron Shed for four cows with Fodder Store at end. Adjoining the Garden also is a brick built and slated GARDENER'S COTTAGE with four rooms.

Except for the cottage, most of these backsheds are now derelict. There is also a centrally placed dipping pond, shown on the map as 'Fn' and until recently, much overgrown.

In 1909 the estate had been sold to a Mr. J. Collett-Mason, and it was he who sold it to the Hereford Council in 1920, when the house and outbuildings were converted into a sanitorium for tuberculosis patients. It appears that the garden continued to be cultivated for producing fruit and vegetables for the patients and staff. John Hope and John Wood both remember the garden in the 1940s; Mr. Hope was a gardener's boy there between 1947 and 1952. Then much of the glass still remained, as did the backsheds, and he recalls the bothy where they ate their sandwiches and dried their clothes by the fire. He also remembers using the wooden door in the south wall as a 'diary', writing in pencil the date when they heard the first call of the cuckoo, or the day on which the potatoes were planted. Sadly these jottings have long since disappeared. Apparently the longer cross path was grassed, whilst the shorter and the perimeter paths were of gravel. He also recollects the various crops that were grown and the layout of the gardens as described in Figure 5, which is based on Mr. Hope's plan. One can speculate that this layout had not changed significantly since the 19th century. Most of the half standards that were grown along the inner side of the perimeter path have long gone, but one or two remain, having grown to an impressive size and in September, heavy with fruit. Cordons were cultivated on either side of the cross paths. Some fruit tree labels of stamped lead remain on the western wall: Thompson's Pear, Black Heart Cherry and Prince Englebert (a black plum), and more were found on the south side of the south wall once the ivy was cleared (Plate II).

Around 1952 the sanitorium was closed and the house was given over to a group of Latvian refugees, who were unable to return to their

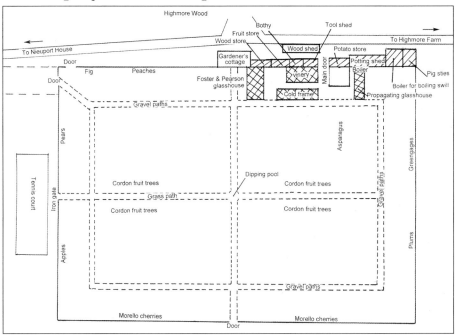

Fig. 5. Plan of garden in the 1940s based on John Hope's description

57

country after the war. The garden continued to be cultivated, albeit in a piece-meal manner, and after the Latvians left in the 1990s little, if any, cultivation took place and it was grassed over. However, overall it is in reasonable condition,

Plate II. 'Prince Englebert',
lead fruit label on the west wall

and the walls are all standing, although until recently they were smoth-ered in ivy. The backsheds are derelict and as mentioned earlier, only one glasshouse remains. The cottage was lived in until recently.

The garden has since been returned to private ownership and the new owners, Mr. and Mrs. David Crichton-Watt, are intent on restoring the garden to its former glory. Already the ivy has been removed and the internal walls re-built and re-pointed (Plate III) in the traditional manner, using lime mortar and hand-made bricks. The ground has been cleared of undergrowth to uncover the paths, as well as most of the glasshouse and frame footings. The weeds and nettles growing in the dipping pond have been removed to reveal a brick-lined pond about five feet deep, complete with an inlet pipe and drain. Fruit trees have been planted against all the walls trained as fans, espaliers and cordons. The local forge has created some arches to support more fruit trees as well as roses, wisteria and laburnum.

Plate III. The new west wall

It is indeed heartening to see such a restoration take place, and to witness the once neglected garden being brought back to life in a way that at the same time respects its history. It will be fascinating to follow the progress of this restoration, and good to see fruit and vegetables being grown there once again.

Donald Beaton and the Walled Garden at Haffield

In 1813 the land that was to form the Haffield estate was separated off from the Hazle estate and within two years its new owner, William Gordon (1794-1836), had commissioned Sir Robert Smirke (1781-1861) to design a villa. Haffield lies three miles south of Ledbury almost at the junction of the Herefordshire and Gloucestershire borders, and just seven miles from Hope End where John Claudius Loudon (1783-1843) was advising on the development of the parkland from around 1810 to 1815.[1] Loudon and Donald Beaton (1802-63), who is believed to have been Haffield's first Head Gardener, were fellow Scots, and Gordon's immediate family also lived in Scotland.[2] Loudon and Beaton clearly knew and trusted each other for in 1837, whilst Beaton was still working at Haffield, Loudon sent him a copy of his paper on the *Amarlyllidaceae* family asking him to write a review of it for a forthcoming issue of the *Gardener's Magazine.*[3] All of this leaves us to ponder whether Loudon may have offered Gordon advice on the purchase of the Haffield site or the early design of the grounds. Gordon certainly had great aspirations for Haffield for in 1820 Uvedale Price (1747-1829) wrote from Foxley, Herefordshire to his good friend, Sir George Beaumont, explaining that:

> Miss Wingfield … is on the point of being married to Mr Gordon who has lately built a house on a spot which must have been, by the account of the last possessor, extremely interesting: he told me there were a number of old yews + fine old pollard oaks on it, but the property being then scattered, + not thinking of it's ever being made a place … he cut them all down 'at one fell swoop,' the yews for gateposts, the pollards for firewood. Mr Gordon, I believe

never saw them … I regret them I believe much more than he does; for I am likely to visit him, + should have had a great delight in seeing them…I am very sorry for them on another account: he means to employ Gilpin, who when he hears the melancholy tale will regret them as much as I do, + for the same reasons.[4]

This was William Sawrey Gilpin (1761/2-1843), nephew of the Revd. Gilpin, the author of *Observations on the River Wye,* and a well respected improver in the Picturesque mould. He was noted for his sensitive handling of trees in the landscape, and published *Practical Hints for Landscape Gardening* in 1832. There is no direct evidence that either Loudon or W.S. Gilpin[5] or Loudon[6] advised Gordon at Haffield although the siting of the house and the design of the walled garden was clearly overseen by someone possessing considerable knowledgeable and experience.

The walled garden at Haffield, of between three and four acres, is presumed to date from the same period as the house and it combines practicality with some more unusual design features. It is located on the lower south-east facing slopes of Haffield Bank, just a few hundred yards from the house. The site uses the slope to maximise the warming effect of

Plate I. The peach house today is used for growing tomatoes

the sun and discourage frosts. Indeed it satisfies Loudon's requirements for the placement of a kitchen garden very well for he declared that it should be, 'as near the mansion and stable-offices, as is consistent with beauty, convenience and other arrangements' and on 'a gentle declivity towards the south, a little inclining towards the east to receive the benefits of the morning sun.'[7] The forcing pits, now used without their lights to grow cabbages, and the Peach House, now used to raise tomatoes, are similarly placed to make the most of the south-east slope (Plate I).[8]

Haffield is notable for being a double walled garden, with one rectangle offset within the other. The long south-east facing wall of the inner rectangle stretches outwards to meet the outer wall and this T-shaped extension supports the main glasshouse. The walls of the outer rectangle are largely constructed of local stone. The walls of the inner rectangle and its T-shaped extension are of more expensive brick, whilst the south-west facing wall of the outer garden has a double skin of brick on the inside and stone on the outside. This brick addition to the outer walls provides a south-west aspect, favourable for fruit growing which is better served by brick than stone, as it retains the warmth longer and provides a natural grid of mortar to carry the nails and wires necessary for espaliers and cordons. The fruit developing on this outer wall was also closest to the watchful eye of the Head Gardener, whose cottage still stands immediately adjacent to it. Another unusual double walled garden existed at Middleton Hall, Carmarthenshire and was restored during the recent establishment of the National Botanic Garden of Wales.

An unusual serpentine tunnel shrouds the approach from the house into Haffield's walled garden. Two Derbyshire gardens, Calke Abbey, now owned by the National Trust, and Chatsworth, also have tunnels. At Chatsworth it carried the coal to the glasshouses and at Calke Abbey the neat brick-lined tunnel led directly into the area containing the 'back sheds,' keeping gardeners out of sight of those enjoying the nearby pleasure gardens. But at Haffield the very different style of the tunnel confirms that it was intended for visitors not workers. It is located in the south-east wall, as far away from the back sheds as it could possibly be, and directly in line with the approach from the house. Loudon held that the entrance to any walled garden should ideally be from the south so that the initial view presented was of the largest, most impressive northern walls complete with their glasshouses, frames and pits (Plate II).[9] The carefully serpentined Haffield tunnel follows these principles

Plate II. The main glasshouse seen on first entering the walled garden with the surviving walls of the cold frame in the foreground

Plate III. The gardener's entrance to the walled garden alongside the lane

precisely, but it adds to the spectacle by emerging from between ivy-clad rocks guarded by two, now mature yews trees, in what is a deliberately composed Picturesque entrance suggestive of W.S. Gilpin's aesthetic. The tunnel is lined with the same chocolate-coloured breccia stone used to build the outer walls. It was mined on the estate and is something of a geological curiosity, being similar to a conglomerate, but composed of angular rather than rounded fragments. Geology was one of the newly emerging sciences that captured the popular interest during the early decades of the 19th century and in 1856, Shirley Hibberd was still advising his readers that 'mineralogical ornaments must be capable of yielding some items of amusement and instruction' in the garden.[10] At Haffield the tunnel into the walled garden provided just such a geological and Picturesque diversion for William Gordon's guests as well as conducting them under the lane that skirted the walled garden on its way to the Gardener's Cottage (Plate III).

Sandwiched between Haffield's double walls is the main south-east facing glasshouse of early 20th-century design that occupies the site of an earlier glasshouse that can be traced on the 1891 Ordnance

Plate IV. Interior of the potting shed

Survey map. Behind it lie the chain of stores and sheds that still house two branding irons, one lettered 'HAFFIELD' and the other 'GARDEN', that were used to mark boxes of produce and tools (Plate IV). The glasshouse is sub-divided into two; one half is still heated, although not by the original hot water pipes installed by the long established glasshouse manufacturer, W.D. Bailey, 272 Holborn, London.[11] Today the unheated portion shelters tender ornamentals and the heated half has vines that produce both green and black dessert grapes (Plates V & VI). A collection of pelargoniums climb the back wall in much the same way they might have done when Beaton was Head Gardener between 1829 and 1837, for he was fascinated by the new science of plant breeding, developing a group of hugely fashionable

Plate V. Ornamentals in the glasshouse

Plate VI. Vines in the glasshouse

zonal pelargoniums known as Nosegays. At least one of these, P. 'Scarlet Nosegay', is still available from nurseries today.

Beaton arrived at Haffield having previously worked as foreman gardener on Sir William Cumming Gordon's estate, Altyre in Moray-shire, and at the Caledonian Horticultural Society in Edinburgh.[12] At Altyre he worked alongside James Sinclair (1809-81) who, like Beaton, went on to develop an important horticultural career, although his was on the international stage.[13] It was also at Altyre that Beaton, 'first began crossing bedding plants and bulbs.'[14] This fascination with plant fertili-sation and hybridisation stayed with him throughout his career. Beaton used his time as Haffield's Head Gardener as a springboard to develop a flourishing horticultural career. During his eight years at Haffield Gordon allowed him considerable freedom to travel, and Beaton recorded annual summer visits to London and, in just one year's round of excursions, visits to some of the foremost gardens in England including Briton Hall (prob-ably Bretton Hall, West Yorkshire); Chatsworth, Derbyshire; Wentworth Woodhouse, South Yorkshire; Broughton (Broughton Hall, North Yorkshire); Dropmore, Buckinghamshire and more locally, Downton

Castle, Herefordshire. He only left Haffield when William Gordon died suddenly at the age of 41, moving to Shrubland Park, Suffolk to take up the prestigious post of Head Gardener at a time when these gardens were being remodelled by Sir Charles Barry (1795-1860). Beaton went on to become one of a small group of Head Gardeners whose influence flourished under the spotlight of 19th-century gardening magazines.[15] He retired from Shrubland Park to devote himself fulltime to his career as a horticultural journalist and breeder of plants in a glasshouse that he christened his 'experimental'.[16]

During his time at Haffield we know that Beaton 'fruited and proved forty-six sorts of Grapes, from all parts of Europe, in a house for the purpose'[17], probably on the same spot where grapes continue to be grown today although in a note that might challenge modern ideas of global warming, he described his grapes as 'the finest out-door grapes I have ever seen'.[18] Beaton's outdoor grapes were not a new departure, for his own research revealed that during the early 18th century Jacob Tonson (1655/6-1736) had owned a successful vineyard that flourished on land incorporated within the Haffield estate boundary.[19] Today the Haffield vines are somewhat unusually planted with their roots inside the walls of the 20th-century glasshouse rather than outside as is the more conventional approach.

It seems inevitable that Beaton also grew pineapples at Haffield for they continued to be a popular kitchen garden fruit in the first half of the 19th century as bulk imported sources only began to infiltrate English fruit markets slowly from around 1820.[20] Also, on one of his garden tours, Beaton had noted that pineapples were being grown on 'dry shelves' at nearby Downton Castle.[21] This is unusual as pineapples were generally grown in a humid atmosphere and in a heated planting bed made up of tanner's bark. We can only speculate that Beaton grew pineapples at Haffield in the forcing pits excavated into the slope immediately in front of the main glasshouse.

We do know that the walled garden at Haffield was, as was usually the case, reserved for the production of the more valuable fruit and vegetable crops. But Beaton also provided the Gordon family with the more basic staples for he described planting potatoes on the estate in an as yet unidentified boggy situation where he had already established trees suited to the environment such as alder, willow and black poplar. He grew potatoes on this spot for three years to 'effectively clean it from weeds, without hurting the progress of the trees, notwithstanding all that has been written to the contrary.'[22] These concluding challenging words which were published in the *Gardener's Magazine*, give some credence to Charles Darwin's observation that Beaton was 'a clever fellow and a damned cocksure man'.[23] This temperament together with Beaton's undoubted skill would have ensured that Haffield's unusual walled garden was well known in its day.

We know far less about Haffield under its second owner, Dr. William Charles Henry (1804-92), and under Beaton's successors as Head Gardener, although we do know that Henry maintained a keen interest in the gardens, planting a Wellingtonia avenue that is visible from within the walled garden as well as many American conifers (Plate VII).[24] Henry was a scientist and a Fellow of the Royal Society who would presumably have shared Beaton's interest in the new scientific developments that were gripping horticulture in the 19th century. During his 55 years at Haffield Henry researched and wrote the biography of his mentor and friend, the scientist John Dalton (1766-1844), who today is most often remembered for unravelling the relationship between the chemical elements that comprise the Periodic Table that still bears his

*Plate VII. Dr William Henry's Wellingtonia avenue
seen from within the walled garden*

name.[25] Coincidentally both of Haffield's 19th-century owners, William Henry and William Gordon, are commemorated in adjacent stained glass windows in the south aisle of St. Michael and All Angels Church, Ledbury.

Today Haffield's walled garden continues to produce vegetables, fruits and flowers for the house. It has an air of abundance, beauty, continuity and romance that is rare amongst such labour-intensive gardens. The house and gardens are private and are not open to the public.

Lugwardine Court Walled Garden

Lugwardine Court is located to the east of Hereford city in the village of Lugwardine just off the A438 (SO 548408). The walled garden is visible from the road as you travel over the Lugg Bridge coming from Hereford. The wall to the west runs alongside the road as you travel up into the village.

The earliest history that can be traced for the site is the construction of the existing house for the Revd. John Freeman in 1810, when it was known as Rockfield House (Plate I). He had married Anne Gardiner of Bishops Frome in 1799 and died in 1811, one year after the house was completed. It was his widow and his son, John Gardiner Freeman, who lived in the house for the next half century.

According to the census of 1851, Freeman was then living there with his wife, two children and mother-in-law. However, in his 1866 obituary, John Gardiner Freeman is stated to be of Rock House, just south of the church, and his widow, Mary, was still living in Rock House in 1871.

Plate I. Rockfield House

During the tenure of the Freemans the walled garden was laid out with two asymmetrical paths dividing the garden into unequal quarters and a path around the inside of the walls, as can be seen on an estate map of 1865 (Fig. 1). An open plot stood between the south wall and what is now Tidnor Lane.

By 1868 Sir Herbert George Denman Croft, son of Sir Richard Croft and MP for the county of Hereford from 1868 to 1874, had purchased Lugwardine Court. It was also around this date that he married Georgina Eliza Lucy Marsh.

On the basis of the 1st edition OS map of 1888, it would appear that within the first two decades of their occupation the Crofts dramatically altered the layout of the kitchen garden. It was effectively extended southwards to the road. The lodge had been built on the corner between 1865 and 1888, and a roughly triangular plot assigned to this. The now extended garden was divided into six unequal parts (Fig. 2). Glasshouses and a boilerhouse appear to have been erected on the south-facing north wall. Part of the boilerhouse structure still remains lying between the two greenhouses against the north wall today. These greenhouses were reclaimed from the old Hereford Council nursery site and have been erected where the original glasshouses would have been. There is also evidence of nails in the walls for the tying in of fruit trees, probably peaches that would have needed the protection of glass.

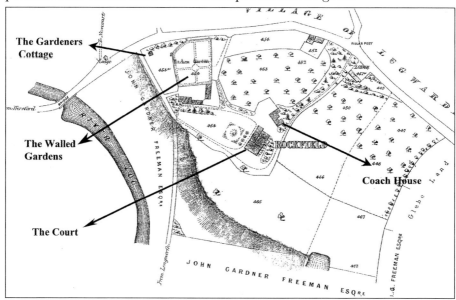

Fig. 1. Estate map, 1865

70

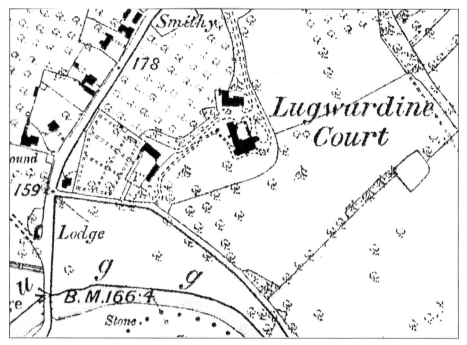

Fig. 2. 1st edition OS map, 1888

Walled gardens of the Victorian period were designed to produce fruits, salads and other vegetables over an artificially prolonged season. By walling in the garden a favourable microclimate was created to achieve this. Brick walls were ideal as they warmed up quickly and retained the heat better than stone. The walls here have been built with rubble stone and faced in part with brick on the inside.

Lugwardine Court later became the home of the Sisters of Charity who established St. Mary's School when they located there in 1954, but in 1986 it was sold and opened as a nursing home. When it came up for sale in 1999, parents, friends and staff of St. Mary's School set about the task of buying the house and land in order to benefit the school and the community. They were successful in their aim and have now set up the Lugwardine Education Centre.

The walled garden has subsequently been leased out to Workmatch with the aim of restoring it as a Victorian-style working kitchen garden. Workmatch is a charitable company and provides training and support for disadvantaged people to help them prepare for and find places in the ordinary work environment. It also provides training placements for the long term unemployed. Funding was obtained to assist Workmatch

71

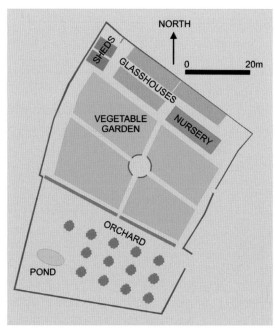

Plate II. Garden plan

Plate III. The cross paths in the garden

in the restoration of the garden, the main funding coming from the Heritage Lottery Fund and Rivers Leader Plus.

The layout of the paths was influenced by the earlier plan, however the paths are not in the exact original position as the current glasshouses now overlay some of the original garden. The new design is based on the plan of the garden shown on the 1865 estate map (Plate II). The garden is entered by a gate in the east wall and is divided into four quarters, with a central feature, typical of walled kitchen gardens of the time (Plate III). Borders along the walls have been planted with fruit trees, small fruit bushes and salad crops.

One of the greenhouses reclaimed from the old council nursery has been split in half to provide two lean-to greenhouses against the south-facing wall. The other has been erected as a free-standing glasshouse (Plate IV). The glasshouses allow room for up to 250 hanging baskets to be made for businesses in Hereford. They also provide space for growing vegetables and over-wintering tender plants. With the completion of the erection of the glasshouses and repairs to the wall, work has moved on to establish the garden as a working kitchen garden. There were some delays to the project owing to the partial collapse of the west wall adjacent to Ledbury Road in the winter of 2005/6.

The aim of the development of the garden is to make it as attractive as possible for visitors and to make the best use of the available space in order to provide a variety of activities for the trainees who come to the garden for work experience. Two long borders have been planted up with herbaceous plants and roses along the west wall. Not only will this look attractive but it will also provide plant material for the trainees to learn about propagation. Pergolas have been erected as supports for roses and clematis and a small herb garden has been established. Trainees can learn about plant maintenance and pruning techniques. They also learn about health and safety in the workplace and are trained in the use of garden machinery.

Old varieties of vegetables are grown such as the potatoes Pink Fir Apple (1850) and Belle de Fontenay (1885). Tomatoes come in all sorts of shapes and sizes, and include Pink Brandywine, an Amish variety

Plate IV. The greenhouses

73

known in America since 1887, and Black Russian. Another idea is to start growing some of the older varieties of garden plants and flowers for cutting. Victorian kitchen gardens would have grown a lot of flowers for cutting for the house; popular varieties included sweet peas, asters and antirrhinums. Visitors to the project will therefore see much to interest them as well as being able to sample different types of vegetables not usually available in the shops.

The project is run as a business to provide much needed income. Income is generated from the sale of hanging baskets, vegetables and plants. A number of open days have been held for visitors to see the project and to buy plants. The garden also acts as a base from which garden maintenance contracts are carried out in the area; this also provides further experience for the trainees.

The project is working closely with the Lugwardine Education Centre and St. Mary's School (a specialist science school), as part of a wider scheme to develop Lugwardine Court into a unique learning and visitor resource for the benefit of the local community.

Herefordshire's Surviving Walled Gardens

This list of walled gardens in Herefordshire is derived from David Whitehead's *A Survey of Historic Parks & Gardens in Herefordshire* (2001), from work carried out by Herefordshire Council and from information supplied by members of the Hereford and Worcester Gardens Trust. The editor cannot guarantee the accuracy of the entries and apologises for the inevitable omissions. The Gardens Trust would be delighted to hear from any readers who might be able to add to the list.

Please note that this list does not imply that gardens are open to the public. Those that we know are open are so described and similarly those that are known to be private. The rest must be assumed to be private.

	Property	Civil Parish	Condition	Use, if known	Any other comments
1	Abbey Dore Court	Abbey Dore	excellent	flower garden	open to public
2	Aconbury Court	Aconbury	reduced in places	pasture	medieval stone
3	Allensmore Court	Allensmore	fragmentary	pasture	private
4	Aramstone	King's Caple	good	flowers	open occasionally
5	Bartestree Court	Bartestree	overgrown		
6	Barton Court	Colwall	excellent	flowers and vegetables	private
7	Belmont House	Belmont Rural	well maintained walls	new house and garden	private
8	Berrington Hall	Eye, Moreton and Ashton	good but glass houses have gone, bothy and potting sheds to restore	orchard and flower garden	English Heritage Registered garden, National Trust, open to public

	Name	Parish	Condition	Use	Notes
9	Bircher Hall	Croft, Yarpole and Bircher	poor	multiple use	massive stone buttresses, unusual construction
10	Birchyfield	Avenbury	derelict	overgrown	
11	Bodenham Manor	Bodenham	poor	new buildings in garden, some cultivation	a special school
12	Bollitree Castle	Weston-under-Penyard	well maintained walls	new house and garden	private
13	Bosbury House	Bosbury	well used	kitchen garden	private
14	Brampton Bryan	Brampton Bryan	good	orchard	English Heritage Registered garden, extensive walled garden
15	Bredenbury Court	Bredenbury			now a school
16	Broadfield Court	Bodenham	good	fruit, vegetables and flowers	open to public
17	Brobury House, (Quinta)	Brobury with Monnington-on-Wye	good	mainly laid to lawn	private
18	Brockhampton Park	Brockhampton (near Bromyard)	excellent	glasshouses converted to house	private walled garden English Heritage Registered park owned by National Trust

					English Heritage Registered garden
19	Broxwood Court	Pembridge	excellent	formal, ornamental garden	English Heritage Registered garden
20	Bryan's Ground	Stapleton	variable, walls need some attention	cottage garden	open to public
21	Bryngwyn	Much Dewchurch	poorly maintained	mainly grassed over	house in multiple ownership
22	Buckenhill	Norton	most of wall intact	grassed over	
23	Buckland	Docklow and Hampton Wafre		grassed over	
24	Burton Court	Eardisland	falling down	pasture	
25	Burton Court	Linton (near Ross)	good	lawns and shrubbery	
26	Byletts	Pembridge	standing	house inside	
27	Canon Frome Court	Canon Frome	poor	partly derelict	walls need urgent attention, glass derelict
28	Canon Pyon House	Canon Pyon	only half the walls standing	now part of an open cultivated field	
29	Caradoc	Sellack	poor	vegetable garden	walls need re-pointing
30	Castle Weir	Lyonshall	good		walls have been reduced in height
31	Chadnor Court	Dilwyn	poor, walls partially intact	grassed over	part of working farm

32	Clater Park	Linton (near Bromyard)	walls restored	grassed over	private, elliptical garden with gothic bothy
33	Coddington Court	Coddington	walls partially intact and in good condition	lawns and shrub beds	special needs school
34	Court of Noke	Pembridge	good	flower garden	private
35	Courtfield	Welsh Bicknor	poor	unused, some surviving soft fruits	recent addition of door to gateway
36	Credenhill Court	Credenhill	poor, only part of two walls remain	grassed over	
37	Croft Castle	Croft, Yarpole and Bircher	good	orchard, vineyard and ornamental planting	English Heritage Registered garden, collection of historic apple varieties
38	Dingwood	Ledbury Rural	walls intact	domestic garden	private
39	Donnington Hall	Donnington	good	grassed over	vinery in good condition
40	Downton Castle	Downton	excellent	fruit, vegetables	English Heritage Registered garden, glasshouses now restored
41	Dulas Court	Dulas	poor to fair	3 walls only intact	Victorian house along 4th side
42	Eastnor Castle	Eastnor	variable	variable	glass gone, English Heritage Registered garden
43	Easton Court	Little Hereford	walls need some repair	laid to grass with trees and shrubs	range of bothies is intact

	Name	Location	Condition	Garden	Notes
44	**Eaton Hall**	Leominster	walls intact	fruit, vegetables and flower garden	
45	**Eccleswall Court**	Linton	walls intact	small quartered garden laid to grass	
46	**Eye Manor**	Eye, Moreton and Ashton	good	ornamental garden	private
47	**Eyton Old Hall**	Eyton	derelict	overgrown	English Heritage Registered garden
48	**Eywood**	Titley	derelict	overgrown	English Heritage Registered garden
49	**Foxley**	Yazor	walls excellent	cider apple orchards	
50	**Gaines**	Whitbourne		laid to lawn	
51	**Garnons**	Mansell Gamage	very good	ornamental	English Heritage Registered garden, orchard, tennis court
52	**Garnstone**	Weobley	derelict	overgrown	
53	**Gayton Hall**	Upton Bishop	unused	grassed over	
54	**Glewstone Court**	Marstow	little remaining of walls	ornamental grounds	now a hotel
55	**Goodrich Court**	Goodrich	fair, walls need some repair	mainly grass, some vegetable cultivation	hazel walk recently replanted, cinder path uncovered, `in poor condition, no glass

56	Great Camdore Farm	Orcop	three walls surviving, in need of repair	productive kitchen garden	owners intend to restore/rebuild the walls
57	Grendon Court	Upton Bishop	walls partially intact	domestic garden	
58	Haffield	Donnington	walls need some repair	orchard, kitchen and flower garden and partly grassed over	large garden with interesting tunnel entrance, glass & boilers extant
59	Hagley Park/Court	Lugwardine	mainly destroyed		only one section remains, development
60	Hall Court	Much Marcle	needs restoration	unusual survival of 17th c. flower garden 1608-10	built retrospectively in the Elizabethan style
61	Hampton Court	Hope-under-Dinmore	good	part productive and part ornamental	open to public
62	Harewood Park	Harewood	poor, walls need re-bonding; glass derelict	grassed over, derelict buildings	earlier walled garden gone, remaining garden is later
63	Heath House	Leintwardine	reasonable	flower garden	
64	Hennor House	Leominster	good	productive kitchen garden	
65	Highwood House	Croft, Yarpole and Bircher	poor	uncultivated	

No.	Name	Parish	Condition	Use	Notes
66	Hill Court	Walford	excellent	formal ornamental garden	English Heritage Registered garden
67	Hoe Court	Colwall	poor	partly derelict	range of sheds and bothy intact
68	Holme Lacy	Holme Lacy	walls good	non productive (save wall fruit), tennis court, accommodation.	hotel, English Heritage Registered garden
69	Holmer Park	Holmer and Shelwick	wall intact	now housing	
70	Homend	Stretton Grandison		ornamental garden	
71	Homme House	Much Marcle	poor, glass derelict	large	English Heritage Registered garden, Grade 1 listed gazebo under renovation
72	Hope End	Colwall	excellent	vegetables and flowers	English Heritage Registered garden, new house in walled garden
73	John Kyrle's Garden	Ross-on-Wye	still there	ornamental garden	new house in top garden
74	Kentchurch Court	Kentchurch	poor, walls need re-pointing	partially used for vegetables	English Heritage Registered garden, glasshouse in process of restoration

75	**Kinnersley Castle**	**Kinnersley**	average, walls and paths need rebuilding, glass derelict	fruit and vegetables	interesting Dutch influenced design with 'ante room'
76	**Kinsham Court**	**Kinsham**		productive kitchen garden	
77	**Knill Court**	**Knill**	good	laid to lawn	
78	**Langstone Court**	**Llangarron**	good	flower garden	open to public
79	**Lawton Hall**	**Eardisland**	only 1 wall remains, grand scale	unused	owners intend to restore
80	**Letton Court**	**Letton**	good	cultivated	
81	**Lewis Wych/The Whittern**	**Lyonshall**	good	productive kitchen garden	
82	**Longworth**	**Lugwardine**	poor	partly derelict	walls & glass derelict
83	**Lower Eaton**	**Eaton Bishop**	walls partially survive	grassed over	
84	**Lugwardine Court**	**Lugwardine**	recently restored	vegetable garden and education	provides work opportunity for disabled
85	**Lynhales**	**Lyonshall**	derelict	overgrown	
86	**Marden Court**	**Marden**	good	domestic garden	site of modern house

87	Michaelchurch Court	Michaelchurch Escley	partial, only two walls were ever constructed	ornamental garden	
88	Moccas Court	Moccas	walls fair to good	filled with previously planted and uncropped conifers	English Heritage Registered garden, well documented, walls and doors good, plunge pool and paths gone.
89	Moor Court	Pembridge	good	domestic garden	new house built outside the wall
90	Moor House, Widemarsh Common	Hereford City	walls partially intact	partially cultivated	
91	Moraston House	Bridstow	good	vegetables, fruit and flowers	private kitchen garden
92	New Court	Lugwardine	walls intact and fair condition	partially overgrown	
93	Nieuport House	Almeley	fair	in process of restoration	English Heritage Registered garden, walls being rebuilt, one glasshouse remaining
94	Old Colwall	Colwall	variable to good	ornamental and vegetables	series of walled gardens, glasshouses need restoring, 18th c. Barrett Browning connection, adjoins Hope End

95	Old Sufton	Mordiford	average	under grass	small ovoid garden on sloping site, early 18c summer-house/dovecot
96	Pengethley	Sellack	good	hotel garden and vineyard	
97	Pennoxstone Court	King's Caple	poor	only sections of two walls remaining	now occupied by polytunnels
98	Perrycroft	Colwall	poor	vegetables	derelict glass
99	Perrystone Court	Foy	excellent	productive kitchen garden	range of sheds and bothy restored
100	Pontrilas Court	Kentchurch	good, walls and glasshouses surviving	productive kitchen garden	
101	Poulstone Court	King's Caple	some repair needed	three walls standing	grassed over
102	Priors Court	Wellington Heath	good	flower garden	holiday lets
103	Priory Farm	Clifford	walls intact but need repair	grassed over	
104	Pudleston Court	Pudlestone	excellent, walls and glasshouses restored	productive kitchen and formal ornamental gardens	private
105	Pudleston Rectory	Pudlestone	good	kitchen garden and tennis court	

106	**Putley Court**	Putley	good – 2 sides	terraced flower garden	late 18th c. summerhouse
107	**Pyon House**	Canon Pyon	poor	partially demolished	divided ownership, polytunnels
108	**Rotherwas Park**	Dinedor	damaged, but most there	fruit trees, pasture, gardener's cottage	18th c. focus for house
109	**Rudhall House**	Ross Rural	walls need some repair	partly grassed over	
110	**Saltmarshe Castle**	Edvin Loach and Saltmarshe	poor	development	caravan site, walls partly demolished
111	**Sarnesfield Court**	Sarnesfield	walls need repair	grassed over	originally only three walls, most of these remain but in poor condition
112	**Seedley House**	Leintwardine	excellent	productive walled garden	new house built adjacent to garden
113	**Sellarsbrook Park**	Whitchurch	good	ornamental garden	
114	**Shobdon Court**	Shobdon	walls need re-pointing in places	grass and gardens	English Heritage Registered garden, dovecote
115	**Staunton Park**	Staunton-on-Arrow	high walls, mid 18th c.	not used	many buildings
116	**Stoke Edith**	Stoke Edith	intact but walls need repair	partially overgrown, subdivided by hedges	English Heritage Registered garden
117	**Street Court**	Kingsland	good	flower garden	hotel & conference centre

118	**Stretfordbury**	Leominster	poor	partly derelict	
119	**Sufton Court**	**Mordiford**	walls need re-pointing in places	grass and gardens	English Heritage Registered garden, boundary replaced with hedge
120	**Sugwas Court**	**Stretton Sugwas**	poor	overgrown	
121	**Summerhill Park (The Moor)**	**Clifford**	intact walls and remains of paths	grassed over	garden standing on its own in agricultural land
122	**Sutton Court**	**Sutton**	partly cultivated, glasshouses in need of repair	vegetables and flowers	some celebrated Backhouse daffodils still surviving
123	**Tedstone Court**	**Tedstone Delamere**	good	orchard and kitchen garden	
124	**The Great House**	**Canon Pyon**	walls partially intact	productive kitchen garden	private
125	**The Groom's Cottage**	**Ledbury**		domestic garden	
126	**The Hermitage**	**Burghill**		partly cultivated	
127	**The Homme**	**Dilwyn**	walls in poor repair	occupied by modern barns	
128	**The Knoll**	**Bircher**		ornamental domestic garden	
129	**The Mynde**	**Much Dewchurch**	excellent	vegetables	private

No.	Name	Location	Walls	Garden use	Notes
130	The Ryelands	Leominster		domestic garden	divided into two with a house in each part
131	The Vern	Bodenham		one garden derelict, one ornamental flower garden	two walled gardens
132	The Weir (New Weir)	Kenchester	walls on three sides, very poor, need restoring	partly derelict	National Trust has restored glasshouse
133	The Whittern	Lyonshall	good	productive kitchen garden	large garden, sheds and bothy intact
134	Thing-hill	Withington	traces remain	arable	
135	Tidnor Court	Lugwardine	walls need repair	not cultivated	
136	Tillington Court	Burghill	average, walls need re-pointing	private flower and vegetable garden	double walled garden
137	Titley Court	Titley	good	fruit and vegetables	nice little peach house
138	Treago	St Weonard's	good	mixed use	detached from house
139	Tyberton Court	Tyberton	walls and sheds intact but need some repair	large, productive kitchen garden	
140	Underdown	Ledbury	good	grassed over	walls OK, no glass
141	Upleadon Court	Bosbury	walls partially intact	productive kitchen garden	

No.	Name	Parish	Wall condition	Garden use	Notes
142	Upper Hall	Ledbury	most of the wall survives	now housing	private
143	Upper Wintercott	Leominster	walls intact	domestic garden	
144	Upper Wythall	Walford	reasonable, walls need attention	flower garden	domestic garden adjoining 16thc. manor house
145	Vennwood	Bodenham	walls need restoring	productive kitchen garden	recent wall collapse
146	Walford Court	Walford	walls need repair	cultivated kitchen garden	
147	Warham House	Breinton	poor	partially overgrown	
148	Wessington Court	Woolhope	walls and sheds intact	productive kitchen garden	double walled garden, no glass
149	Weston Hall	Weston-under-Penyard	excellent – old bricks 16th c.	fine ornamental garden, fruit vegetables and flowers	new summer house, open for Red Cross events
150	Whitbourne Hall	Whitbourne	fair to good	divided into 'allotments'	restored Foster and Pearson vinery
151	Whitfield	Treville	excellent	Ginkgo biloba is possibly a champion	English Heritage Registered garden, original camellia house
152	Wilcroft	Lugwardine	walls need repair	partly overgrown	some cultivation, polytunnels
153	Winforton House	Willersley and Winforton	walls substantially intact	partially cultivated, vegetables	

154	Withington Court	Withington	poor	domestic garden	
155	Wisteston Court	Marden	fragmentary	abandoned	attached to house
156	Wormsley Grange	Brinsop and Wormsley	good, flower garden from 1740s	ornamental flower garden	house and garden recently restored
157	Wyastone Leys	Ganarew	poor	derelict	

Further Reading

Campbell, S. (1987) *Cottesbrooke, an English Kitchen Garden*
        Century Hutchinson Ltd
        (1998) *Walled Kitchen Gardens*. Shire Publications Ltd
        Buckinghamshire.
        (2005) *A History of Kitchen Gardening* Frances Lincoln Ltd
Davies, J. (1991) *The Victorian Kitchen Garden* BBC Books
Hall, Lois (ed) (2003) *Staffordshire Walled Kitchen Gardens*
        Staffordshire Gardens & Parks Trust
Hix, John (1996) *The Glass House* Phaidon
Lemmon, K. (1972) *The Covered Garden* Museum Press
Lyte, Charles (1984) *The Kitchen Garden* Oxford Illustrated Press
Morgan, J., & Richards, A. (1990) *A Paradise out of a Common Field*
        Century Publishing
Petherick, T. & Eclare, M. (2006) *The Kitchen Gardens at Heligan – Lost*
        Gardening
Principles Discovered Weidenfield & Nicolson
Stuart, David (1984) *The Kitchen Garden, a historical guide to traditional crops*
        Robert Hale
Thompson, Robert (1859) *The Gardener's Assistant* Blackie
Whitehead, David (2001) *A Survey of Historic Parks and Gardens in*
        Herefordshire Hereford and Worcester Gardens Trust
Wilson, C.A. (1998) *The Country House Kitchen Garden, 1600-1950* Alan
        Sutton Publishing Ltd

Endnotes

1 George Skippe and his Walled Garden at Upper Hall, Ledbury

1. Hereford City Library, Woolhope Strong Box W920. The diary was investigated by T.W.M. Johnson, 'The Diary of George Skippe of Ledbury' in *Transactions of the Woolhope Naturalists Field Club (TWNFC)* XXX11 (1953), pp. 54-62.
2. Joe Hillaby, *The Book of Ledbury* (1982), pp. 11-14 and much else on the Skippe family.
3. C.W. & A.J. Johnson, *A History of Upper Hall, Ledbury* (1997), pp. 4-8.
4. William Bray (ed.), *The Diary of John Evelyn* (1895), pp. 454-5.
5. A family tree is produced in Charles Robinson, *The Mansions and Manors of Herefordshire* (1872), p. 170.
6. Johnson, 'Diary', *TWNFC* (1953), p. 55 notes that there is a Bowling Green Cottage in Ledbury.
7. J.A. Wright, *Brickbuilding in England* (1972), p. 393.
8. F.C. Morgan,'The Accounts of St Katherine's Hospital, Ledbury 1584-1595' in *TWNFC* XXXIII (1953), pp. 101, 104, 122-3.
9. Hereford Cathedral Library, Fabric Accounts – Matthew, William and John Fisher were working from c.1663-c.1740. Whilst in Worcester (from various ecclesiastical and municipal sources) Richard, Francis and Henry Richards were active between c.1640 –c.1678 – Pat Hughes, 'Sixteenth and Seventeenth Century Worcester Craftsmen', MSS copy in Worcester Record Office.
10. Both in the Hereford Record Office and copies in the possession of Mr. C. Johnson.
11. Hanging in the main hall at Upper Hall.
12. Quoted by Susan Campbell, 'Digging, Sowing and Cropping in the open Ground, 1600-1900' in C. Anne Wilson (ed.), *The Country House Kitchen Garden 1600-1950* (1998), p. 18.
13. David Whitehead, *A Survey of Historic Parks and Gardens in Herefordshire* (2001), p. 294.
14. Mile Hadfield, *A History of British Gardening* (1969), pp. 114-16 – quoting John Rea (1665).
15. A substantial part of *The English Gardener* has been reprinted by the Herb Grower Press, Falls Village, Connecticut (1954). This is being used here, but it is unpaginated.
16. Johnson, 'Diary', *TWNFC* (1953), p. 58.
17. Quoted in Eleanour Sinclair Rohde, *The Story of the Garden* (1933), pp. 168-9.
18. David C. Stuart, *The Kitchen Garden* (1984), pp. 70-1.
19. Edward Ball,'Fruit Trees planted by George Skippe and Son (?) at Upper Hall, Ledbury, 1671-1705' in *TWNFC* XXXIV (1954), pp. 268-273.
20. John Evelyn, *Sylva* (1664), pp. 25-27 – for the eulogy on the walnut. Evelyn, however, does not distinguish between the Common and Black varieties.
21. Hillaby, *Ledbury*, p. 78.
22. Johnson, *Upper Hall*, pp. 10-11.
23. Reproduced as an endpaper in Hillaby, *Ledbury*.
24. Johnson, *Upper Hall*, pp. 13-20; Pigot, *Directory* (1835), p. 14.

25. In the possession of Mr. Johnson.

26. *Ibid.*, p. 19.

27. Johnson, *Upper Hall*, pp. 21-5.

28. Nathanial Lloyd, *A History of English Brickwork* (1925), pp. 98-100; R.W. Brunskill, *Brick Building in England* (1990), pp. 36-38.

2 The Walled Gardens at Old Sufton and Sufton Court, Mordiford

1. Charles Robinson, *The Mansions and Manors of Herefordshire* (1872), pp. 212-13.

2. *RCHM Herefordshire* II (1932), p. 145.

3. Hereford Record Office (HRO), 'A true Survey of the parish of Stoke Edith… taken by William Deeley, 1680'.

4. Nathaniel Lloyd, *A History of English Brickwork* (1925), pp. 93-5.

5. Alfred Watkins, 'Herefordshire Pigeon Houses' in *Trans. Woolhope Naturl. Fld. Club (TWNFC)* (1890), p. 15.

6. Peter H. Goodchild, ' "No Phantasticall Utopia, but a reall place". John Evelyn, John Beale and Backbury Hill, Herefordshire' in *Garden History* 19 (1991), pp. 105-127.

7. Nicholas Kingsley, 'Visions of Villas' in *Country Life* 27 October 1988, p. 128.

8. W.H. Cooke, *Collections towards the History of Herefordshire* III (1882), p. 73; Anthony Dale, *James Wyatt*, (1936), p. 27.

9. G. Aylmer & J. Tilly, *Hereford Cathedral: A History* (2000), p. 261.

10. David Whitehead and Ron Shoesmith,, *James Wathen's Herefordshire 1770-1820*, (1994), unpaginated.

11. Repton, Humphrey, 'Sufton Court Red Book', facsimile at HRO BB41; David Whitehead, 'Repton and the Picturesque Debate: The Text of the Sufton Red Book' in *The Picturesque* 1 (1992), pp. 6-17.

12. Jeremy Musson, *The English Manor House*, (Aurum Press, 1999).

3 Downton Castle and its Walled Garden

1. Richard Payne Knight whilst writing *The Landscape* probably honed his ideas with his friend and near neighbour Uvedale Price of Foxley who also produced a similar work entitled *Essays on the Picturesque*. The resultant garden and land-scape layout at Downton Castle was no doubt influenced by the two friends.

2. Inglis-Jones, E., *Peacocks in Paradise* (1990), Gomer Press, Llandysul.

3. Elliott, B., *The Royal Horticultural Society – A History 1804-2004* (2004) Phillimore, Chichester.

4. J.B.W., Some account of the Gardens of Herefordshire, *Gardener's Magazine*, XIV (1838), pp. 209-220.

5. Knight, T.A., Garden Notebook 1798-1821, Hereford Record Office, Bundle 437.

6. A draft register description for English Heritage in 1998 by Dr P.A. Stamper, has a summary of the historic significance of the Downton site.

7. Anon, *The Different Modes of Cultivating the Pine-apple* (1822) Longman, London. The copy in the British Library has a note written in pencil stating "by J.C. Loudon".

8. Letter from T.A. Knight to Sir Joseph Banks of 4 October 1819, Mitchell Library, Sydney.

9. Anderson, J., *A Description of a Patent Hot-house to Which is Added An Appendix, Containing Remarks Upon A Letter from Thomas Andrew Knight Esq. On the Subject of Mr. Forsyth's Plaster* (1803) J. Cumming, London.
10. Knight, T.A., *The Report of a Committee of the Horticultural Society of London Drawn Up at their request by T.A. Knight* (1805) Savage and Easingwold, London.
11. Knight, T.A., A Description of a Forcing-house for Grapes; with observations on the best method of constructing houses for other fruits, *Transactions of the (Royal) Horticultural Society*, I, (1812) pp. 99-102. Dates for volumes of the Transactions are as those given by P.M. Synge, 1954, The Publications of the Royal Horticultural Society, *Journal of the Roy. Hort. Soc.,* LXXIX, 528.
12. Letter from T.A. Knight to G.S. Mackenzie of 1815 in *Memoirs of Caledonian Horticultural Society*, II, pp. 258-260.
13. Knight, T.A., Suggestions for the Improvement of Sir George Mackenzie's Plan for Forcing Houses, *Transactions of the (Royal) Horticultural Society*, 2 (1817) pp. 350-353.
14. Knight, T.A., 'Upon the Culture of the Pine apple, without bark, or other Hot Bed', *Transactions of the (Royal) Horticultural Society*, 4 (1822) pp. 72-78.
15. Knight, T.A., On the Cultivation of the Pineapple, *Transactions of the (Royal) Horticultural Society*, 7 (1830) pp.409-416.
16. Knight, T.A., 1830. op.cit.
17. Royal Horticultural Society Council Minutes 1815-1847
18. Anon., 1822, op. cit.
19. J.B.W., op. cit.
20. Letter from T.A. Knight to A.P. de Candolle of 22 November 1832, Geneva Botanic Garden.
21. An amplification about the details of the founders of the Royal Horticultural Society and Knight's role as given by Elliott (op. cit.) is in Mylechreest, M., 'Thomas Andrew Knight and the Founding of the Royal Horticultural Society', *Garden History*, 12 (2) (1984) pp. 132-137.
22. Knight, T.A., 1805, op.cit.

4 The Walled Garden at Nieuport House, Almeley
1. HRO, E12/F/A111/60
2. HRO, E12/F/A111/69 (16 November 1732)
3. David Whitehead, *Historic Parks and Gardens of Herefordshire* (HWGT, 2001) p.291, see also Harvey, John *Early Nurserymen* (Phillimore,1974)
4. HRO, E12/F/A111/3
5. For a fuller account of these considerations see Susan Campbell *A History of Kitchen Gardening* (Frances Lincoln Ltd, 2005) pp. 23-24.
6. My thanks to Neil Porteous for this.
7. HRO, E12/F/A111/184-194
8. Ibid.
9. Ibid.
10. HRO, G/75/1
11. Stephen Switzer, *The Practical Fruit Gardener being the best and newest method of raising, planting and pruning all sorts of fruit-trees* (the 2nd ed, with plans, 1763) p.312.

12. Thomas Hitt *A Treatise of Fruit-Trees* (3rd ed, 1768) p.32.
13. quoted in R.W.D.Fenn *Walking with a Greyhound* (2002) p. 35.
14. Ibid, p.35.
15. The Rev. Richard Hyett Warner, *Historic memories of the Manor and Parish of Almeley* (1917) p.140.
16. HRO, M5/1/32.
17. Foster and Pearson catalogue, (1909) p.85, with thanks to Susan Campbell.

5 Donald Beaton and the Walled Garden at Haffield

1. John Claudius Loudon, *An Encyclopaedia of Gardening Comprising the Theory and Practice of Horticulture, Floriculture, Arboriculture and Landscape-Gardening*, 2nd edn (London: Longman, Hurst, Rees, Orme, Brown and Green, 1824), p. 1076.
2. Strictly speaking Beaton should be titled the Estate Manager as he described how he had 'management of the estate as well as the garden' at Haffield. D. Beaton, 'Some Account of the Vineyard and Plantations of the Celebrated Jacob Tonson, in 1727, at Haffield, near Ledbury; with a Notice of the Improvements Lately Made, and Now in Progress, at That Place ', *Gardener's Magazine,* 12 (1836), pp. 114-16, D. Beaton, 'My Autobiography', *The Cottage Gardener* (1854), pp. 153-58, p. 157.
3. D. Beaton, 'On Amaryllids', *Journal of the Horticultural Society,* 5 (1850), pp. 132-36, p. 133.
4. Charles Watkin and Ben Cowell, *Letters of Uvedale Price*, (Leeds, Maney Publishing, 2006), p. 290.
5. W.S. Gilpin's link to one other Herefordshire site, Hampton Court, and one Worcestershire site, Hadzor, also remains to be confirmed. Sophieke Piebenga, 'William Sawrey Gilpin (1761/2-1843): Picturesque Improver ' (PhD, University of York, 1995), Appendix.
6. By 1815 Loudon had established his horticultural career publishing three separate horticultural titles as well as advising on the laying out of gardens and estates in Scotland and England.
7. John Claudius Loudon, *An Encyclopaedia of Gardening: Comprising the Theory and Practice of Horticulture, Floriculture, Arboriculture and Landscape-Gardening Including All the Latest Improvements; a General History of Gardening in All Countries; and a Statistical View of Its Present State; with Suggestions for Its Future Progress in the British Isles*, imp. and enlarged edn (London: Longman, Rees, Orme, Brown, Green and Longman, 1834), pp. 719-20.
8. The Peach House is first shown on the 1904 25 inch OS map.
9. Loudon, *Encyclopaedia of Gardening, (1834)*, p. 721.
10. Shirley Hibberd, *Rustic Adornments for Homes of Taste*, Facsimile of 1856 edn (London: Century, 1987), p. 409.
11. Loudon sold his patent for the production of the first wrought iron curvilinear glazing bar to W. D. Bailey in 1818. This had an immense effect on glass house design by narrowing the width of glazing bars and increasing the light levels within. Bailey's erected many of the earliest glasshouses and conservatories around the country including the massive domed Conservatory at Bretton Hall some 100 ft in diameter and 60 ft high. Erected around 1827 it was the largest

of its kind in the world although it was not in use for very long as its two huge boilers struggled to maintain a suitable temperature. Kenneth Lemmon, *The Covered Garden* (London: Museum Press, 1962), p. 141. I am grateful to Fiona Grant for bringing this to my attention.

12. It has been suggested that the names may have been accidentally reversed in Beaton's short autobiography, and this may have been a reference to Sir William Gordon Cumming.

13. Sinclair moved from Altyre to London where he worked for Thomas Andrew Knight (1759-1838), the younger brother of Richard Payne Knight of Downton Castle, Herefordshire, and the President of the Horticultural Society from 1811 to 1838. He went on to become Head Gardanere to Prince Woronzoff at the Aloupka Palace in the Crimea from where, Tsar Nicholas I borrowed him to assist in laying out the Imperial Gardens, St. Petersburg. Sinclair returned to England when the Crimea War broke out then, according to Beaton, he fled to Australia as his specialist knowledge of the layout of Sebastopol made him an obvious target for Turkish and Russian spies. In Australia he established *The Gardener's Magazine and Journal of Rural Economy* and contributed much to the development of Melbourne as a garden city.

14. Beaton, 'My Autobiography', p. 156.

15. Others included Sir Joseph Paxton (1803-65) (Chiswick and Chatsworth), George Fleming (1809-76) (Trentham Hall, Staffordshire), John Fleming (?-1883) (Cliveden, Buckinghamshire) and Zadoc Stephens (*c.*1833-86) (Trentham Hall.)

16. Anon., 'Mr Donald Beaton', *Journal of Horticulture and Cottage Gardener* (1863), p. 266.

17. Beaton, 'My Autobiography', p. 157.

18. Beaton, 'Some Account of the Vineyard', p. 116.

19. Ibid. The long association of this area with vines is still reflected in the name of Haffield's neighbouring farm, The Vineyard. Tonson was a London publisher who made his fortune in publishing John Milton's *Paradise Lost* which he is pictured holding in Sir Geoffrey Kneller's portrait of him painted to record his role as Secretary of the Kit Kat Club. He went on to publish the works of Dryden and Pope supplying Pope with information on John Kyrle whom he celebrated in the *Man of Ross*. I am grateful to David Whitehead for pointing out the connection between Tonson, Pope and the *Man of Ross*.

20. Susan Campbell, *Charleston Kedding* (London: Ebury Press, 1996), David C. Stuart, *The Kitchen Garden: A Historical Guide to Traditional Crops* (London: Robert Hale, 1984), p. 165.

21. Beaton, 'My Autobiography', p. 157.

22. Beaton, 'Some Account of the Vineyard', p. 115.

23. Miles Hadfield, Robert Harling, and Leonie Highton, *British Gardeners: A Biographical Dictionary* (London: A. Zwemmer, 1980), p. 31.

24. Ron Sidwell, *West Midland Gardens* (Stroud: Alan Sutton, 1981), p. 56.

25. William Charles Henry, *Memoirs of the Life and Scientific Researches of John Dalton* (London: n.p., 1854).

Index of Names